Parliament

London: H M S O

Researched and written by Reference Services, Central Office of Information.

HMSO publications are available from:

HMSO Publications Centre
(Mail, fax and telephone orders only)
PO Box 276, London SW8 5DT
Telephone orders 071-873 9090
General enquiries 071-873 0011
(queuing system in operation for both numbers)
Fax orders 071-873 8200

HMSO Bookshops
49 High Holborn, London WC1V 6HB   071-873 0011
Fax 071-873 8200 (counter service only)
258 Broad Street, Birmingham B1 2HE   021-643 3740   Fax 021-643 6510
33 Wine Street, Bristol BS1 2BQ   0272 264306   Fax 0272 294515
9-21 Princess Street, Manchester M60 8AS   061-834 7201   Fax 061-833 0634
16 Arthur Street, Belfast BT1 4GD   0232 238451   Fax 0232 235401
71 Lothian Road, Edinburgh EH3 9AZ   031-228 4181   Fax 031-229 2734

HMSO's Accredited Agents
(see Yellow Pages)

and through good booksellers

Cover photograph credit
COI Pictures.

Contents

Introduction

The system of parliamentary government in Britain[1] is not based on a written constitution, but is the result of gradual evolution over many centuries. The main feature of the system is that government ministers are members of the legislature and are responsible to an elected assembly, the House of Commons, which is made up of representatives from all parts of the country. The Government can only remain in office for as long as it has the support of a majority in the House of Commons, where it has to face public criticism by an Opposition capable of succeeding it as a government should the electorate so decide.

Britain's Parliament is one of the oldest representative assemblies in the world; it is sometimes known as the 'mother of parliaments'. As a result British parliamentary practice has exercised a profound influence on the development of parliamentary institutions overseas, particularly in the other countries of the Commonwealth.

---

[1] The term 'Britain' is used in this booklet to mean the United Kingdom of Great Britain and Northern Ireland; 'Great Britain' comprises England, Wales and Scotland.

The Powers of Parliament

Parliament is the supreme legislative authority in Britain. It is made up of the monarch and the House of Lords and the elected House of Commons. The three elements meet together only on important ceremonial occasions such as coronations, or the State opening of Parliament, when the Commons are summoned by the Queen to the House of Lords. The agreement of all three elements is normally required for legislation, but that of the Queen is given as a matter of course to Bills sent to her.

Parliament can legislate for Britain as a whole or for any part of the country. It can also legislate for the Channel Islands and the Isle of Man, which are Crown dependencies and not part of Britain; they have local legislatures which are subordinate to Parliament and which make laws on island affairs.[2]

Under the Parliament Act 1911 the maximum term of a Parliament is five years (although it may be dissolved and a general election held before the end of this term). If both Houses agree, however, the term can be prolonged without consulting the electorate (as happened during the first and second world wars). Parliament is not subject to the type of legal restraints imposed on the legislatures of countries with formal written constitutions and is thus free to legislate as it pleases, subject to Britain's obligations as a member of the European Union. It may, for instance, make,

[2]The legislatures of the Channel Islands (the States of Jersey and the States of Guernsey) and the Isle of Man (the Tynwald Court) consist of the Queen, the Privy Council and the local assemblies. The Home Secretary, as the Privy Counsellor primarily concerned with island affairs, is responsible for scrutinising each legislative measure before it is submitted to the Queen in Council.

unmake, or alter any law; legalise past illegalities; make void and punishable what was lawful when done and thus reverse the decisions of the ordinary courts; and overturn established conventions[3] or turn them into law.

In practice Parliament does not assert its supremacy in this way. Its members bear in mind the common law which has grown up over the centuries, and normally act in accordance with precedent and tradition. Both Houses are, moreover, sensitive to public opinion. The House of Commons is directly responsible to the electorate, and in this century the House of Lords has recognised the supremacy of the elected chamber. The system of party government in Britain helps to ensure that Parliament legislates with its responsibility to the electorate in mind.

The Crown and Parliament

The legal existence of Parliament depends upon the exercise of the royal prerogative which, broadly speaking, comprises the collection of residual powers left in the hands of the Crown. However, the powers of the Crown[4] in connection with Parliament may be limited and changed by legislation and are always exercised subject to the advice of ministers responsible to Parliament.

As the temporal 'governor' of the established Church of England, the Queen, on the advice of the Prime Minister, appoints the archbishops and bishops. Some, as 'lords spiritual', are members of the House of Lords (see p. 23). As the 'fountain of honour' the Queen confers peerages (on the recommendation of the Prime

[3]Rules and practices which are not part of the law in the sense that violation of them would lead to proceedings in a court of law, but which are regarded nevertheless as vital to the machinery of government.
[4]For further information about the monarchy, see *The Monarchy* (Aspects of Britain: HMSO, 1991).

Minister, who usually seeks the views of others). Thus the 'lords temporal', who form the remainder of the upper House, have likewise been created by Royal prerogative, and their numbers may be increased at any time.

Parliament is summoned by royal proclamation; it is also prorogued (discontinued until the next session) and dissolved by the Queen. At the beginning of each session the Queen drives in state to the House of Lords and opens Parliament in person. (In special circumstances, this may be done by royal commissioners acting on her behalf.) At the opening ceremony the Queen addresses the assembled Lords and Commons. The Queen's speech is written by her ministers and outlines the Government's policies and proposed legislation for the session.

The Sovereign's assent is required before any legislation can take effect—Royal Assent to Bills is now usually declared to Parliament by the Speakers of the two Houses. However, in practice the Sovereign's right to veto has long since fallen into disuse.[5]

Parliamentary Sessions

The life of a Parliament is divided into sessions. Each usually lasts for one year—normally beginning and ending in October or November. A session is usually ended by prorogation, although it may be terminated by dissolution. During a session either House may adjourn, on its own motion, to any date it pleases.

Prorogation usually takes the form of an announcement on behalf of the Queen made in the House of Lords to both Houses. It lasts until a fixed date. The date appointed may be deferred or brought forward by subsequent proclamations. Prorogation

[5]It was last used in 1707, when Queen Anne refused Royal Assent to a Bill for settling the militia in Scotland.

brings to an end nearly all parliamentary business. This means that all public Bills not completed in the session lapse, and have to be reintroduced in the next session unless they are abandoned.

Parliament is usually dissolved by proclamation when a government requests a dissolution, normally before the end of its five-year term. The unbroken continuity of Parliament is assured by the fact that the same proclamation which dissolves the existing Parliament orders the issue of writs for the election of a new one and announces the date on which the new Parliament is to meet. Formerly dissolution followed the death of the Sovereign, but since the Representation of the People Act 1867 the duration of Parliament has been independent of the life of the Sovereign. Should the Sovereign die between the dissolution and the general election, the election and the meeting of the new Parliament would be postponed for 14 days.

Adjournments do not affect uncompleted business. The reassembly of Parliament can be brought forward (if the adjournment was intended to last for more than 14 days) by royal proclamation, or, at short notice if the public interest demands it, by powers specially conferred by each House on its Speaker.

The average number of sitting days for the House of Commons in a normal session is about 160. These are divided into the following periods:

—November till Christmas, lasting about 35 sitting days;

—January to Easter—about 50 sitting days;

—Easter until the late Spring Bank Holiday at the end of May—about 30 sitting days; and

—from about the beginning of June until about late July or early August, lasting about 40 to 50 sitting days.

Nowadays the session is often concluded with a short period in October after the long summer adjournment. During most sessions the House of Lords sits on about 145 days. The periods when Parliament is not sitting are popularly known as 'recesses', although the correct term is 'adjournments'. Parliament also normally adjourns at night and at weekends.

Northern Ireland

Between 1921 and 1972 Northern Ireland had its own Parliament and Government, subordinate to the Parliament at Westminster. In 1972, following several years of intercommunal violence and terrorism, the British Government decided to assume direct responsibility for law and order. The Northern Ireland Government resigned in protest against this decision and direct rule from Westminster began.

This allows the Parliament in Westminster to approve all laws for Northern Ireland and places its government departments under the direction and control of the Secretary of State for Northern Ireland, who is a Cabinet minister. Most legislation formerly carried out by Act of the Northern Ireland Parliament is now considered at Westminster in the form of draft statutory instruments.

Attempts have been made by successive British governments to find a means of restoring a widely acceptable form of devolved government to Northern Ireland. The British Government remains committed to the principle of a locally accountable administration acceptable to, and enjoying the support of, both sections of the community.

In 1991 and 1992 formal talks involving the British Government, the Irish Government and the four main Northern Ireland constitutional parties—the Ulster Unionists, Democratic

Unionists, the Social Democratic and Labour Party and the Alliance Party—ended in November 1992 without full agreement; however further discussions are continuing.

In December 1993 the Prime Minister, John Major, and his Irish counterpart, Albert Reynolds, signed a joint declaration setting out a framework of the political realities and constitutional principles which would inform the search for a political settlement. Both governments pledged that they would seek—together with the Northern Ireland constitutional political parties—to create institutions and structures enabling the people of Ireland to work together in all areas of common interest and to build the trust needed to end past divisions.

The European Union

Britain is a member of the European Union, of which the European Community is a part. Under the provisions of the 1957 Rome Treaty and subsequent treaties, Community legislation consists of legally binding regulations made by the Council of the European Union which comprises government ministers from each member state. The Council also approves directives, each member state's Parliament choosing how to implement them. Members of both Houses of the British Parliament are kept informed by the Government of European Union developments.

The British people, like those in other Union member countries, elect their representatives to the European Parliament, which consists of 567 members (from June 1994) sitting according to party affiliation and not nationality. Britain has 87 of the 567 seats. Elections to the Parliament are held every five years, the most recent taking place in June 1994. Of the British representatives, 71 are elected in England, 8 in Scotland, 5 in Wales and 3 in Northern

Ireland. In England, Scotland and Wales voting is by the simple majority system in large single member constituencies. The three members in Northern Ireland are elected in one constituency by the single transferable vote of proportional representation—the system used there in local government elections.

The franchise and conditions for candidature are broadly the same as for elections to the House of Commons (see p. 32). Unlike Commons elections, peers and clergy of the churches of England, Scotland and Ireland and of the Roman Catholic Church are entitled to stand and to vote.

The European Parliament meets for about one week every month in full session, usually in Strasbourg; its committee work normally takes place in Brussels.

Powers of the Parliament

The European Parliament scrutinises draft legislation, questions members of the Council and debates major policy issues. It also questions members of the European Commission which proposes legislation for decision by the Council.

The Parliament can amend a Commission proposal, give an opinion on the Council's view of certain legislation or reject the Council's position which means that it is reconsidered by the Council.

Under the 1992 Maastricht Treaty the powers of the Parliament have been strengthened on matters like internal market legislation, research and development, trans-European networks, training, education, culture, health, the environment and consumer affairs. This new 'negative assent' procedure begins with the Commission giving a proposal to the Council and the Parliament. The Parliament then gives its opinion and the Council establishes a common position. The Parliament then considers the common position. It can approve it, take no action or reject the common position by an absolute majority. In the event of rejection, the Council can convene a joint Council-Parliament conciliation committee to see if agreement can be reached. If conciliation fails, the Parliament can confirm its rejection of the Council's position, again by an outright majority. This means that the proposal is not accepted.

The Parliament is responsible for formally adopting the Community budget and has the power to reject the budget as a whole.

The Growth of Parliamentary Government

Early Developments in England

The growth of political institutions in England can be traced back to the period of Saxon rule, which lasted from the fifth century AD to the Norman Conquest in 1066. This period saw the origins of the institution of kingship around which the constitution later developed. Moreover, the Saxon kings were advised by a Witenagemot (assembly of the wise), which was continued in a modified form by the Norman kings. The Saxons also established a network of local government areas, including shires (counties) and burghs (boroughs) which continue to influence the structure of local government.

The conquest of England from across the English Channel by Duke William of Normandy (William the Conqueror) marked a turning point in constitutional development. William confiscated the estates of the Saxon earls and divided them among his followers on a feudal basis, so that the tenant's foremost obligation was obedience to the King. He also reconstituted the existing local institutions so that they did not undermine strong, central control; and brought the Church, which played a major role in medieval government, under effective supervision. As a result, William I and his two immediate successors exercised a measure of control never attained by Saxon monarchs. Royal powers were further strengthened during the reign of Henry II (1154–89), who curbed rebellious nobles and churchmen, and transformed locally elected sheriffs into royally appointed central government agents charged with enforcing law and collecting taxes in the counties. He also developed a body of travelling royal judges whose decisions in the cases which came before them gradually evolved into the historic common law.

The Great Council and the Curia Regis

To assist the King in running the Government and in formulating policies two main agencies were developed—the Magnum Concilium, or Great Council, and the Curia Regis, or King's Court. Like the Saxon Witenagemot, the Norman Council included leading men, bishops, officers of the royal household, tenants-in-chief (tenants holding land directly from the King) and others. It met three or four times a year at the summons of the King to help him decide policies of state, to review the work of administration, to sit as a high court of justice, and to take part in making and amending laws.

Originally the Curia Regis was not strictly a separate body. The council met infrequently and for only a few days at a time, and it was found convenient to have the continuing business of the State supervised by a smaller group of members of the council. This consisted of officers of the royal household (for example, the Chamberlain and the Chancellor) who were already accompanying the King wherever he went and were involved in administration. This inner circle of the council constituted the Curia Regis. The King might hold discussions in the council or the curia as he chose and did not have to accept the advice received. Nevertheless the practice of the King calling together his chief subjects, and of relying on them not only for assistance in law-making and administration but for information, opinions and support, was of lasting importance.

Over time the council and the curia grew further apart. As the volume of business in the curia increased, lawyers, financiers and other specialists were drawn in, and during the reign of Henry II a tendency to divide the curia's varied duties into distinct branches developed. Judicial work was gradually separated from general administration, and, while one section of the curia (known as the Permanent Council and later as the Privy Council) continued as a council for general purposes, another evolved into the common law courts.

Magna Carta

The immediate successors of Henry II had difficulty controlling the growing machinery of government. The actions of King John (1199–1216) in particular led to demands by the King's tenants-in-chief, the barons and the leading dignitaries of the Church for redress of their grievances. In 1215, at Runnymede, the barons forced John to agree to a series of concessions set out in a charter, later called Magna Carta (the Great Charter). The charter provided for the protection of the rights of feudal proprietors against the abuse of the royal prerogative. For two centuries, in the course of which it was confirmed many times (the confirmation of 1297 was the earliest enactment in what later came to be known as the Statute Book), it became the authoritative expression of the rights of the community against the Crown. During the next two centuries the charter was virtually neglected, but it was rediscovered in the 17th century, during the struggle between King and Parliament. The Charter thus 'became a bridge between the older monarchy, limited by the restraints of medieval feudalism and the modern constitutional monarchy, limited by a national law enforced by Parliament.'[6]

[6]*Magna Carta Commemoration Essays* (Royal Historical Society, 1917): 'Magna Carta 1215–1915', by W S McKechnie.

Rise of the English Parliament

Medieval kings were expected to meet all royal expenses, private and public, out of their own revenue. If extra resources were needed for an emergency, such as war, the Sovereign would seek to persuade his barons, in the Great Council, to grant an aid. During the 13th century several kings found their private revenues and baronial aids insufficient to meet the expenses of government. They therefore summoned to the Great Council not only their own tenants-in-chief but also representatives of counties, cities and towns, to get their assent to extraordinary taxation. In this way the Great Council came to include those who were summoned by name (the tenants-in-chief) and those who were representatives of communities (the commons). The two parts, together with the Sovereign, eventually became known as 'Parliament'. (The first official use of this term, which originally meant a meeting for parley or discussion, was in 1236.)

The first King known to have summoned knights of the counties to a council was Richard I (1189–99). In 1254 the knights were again summoned and the sheriffs were instructed that the knights were to be elected by the counties and were to represent them in the discussion of what aid should be given to the King 'in his great emergency'. The knights were summoned again in 1261, but by this time civil war had broken out. The leader of the victorious baronial faction, Simon de Montfort, summoned a parliament in 1264 and another in 1265 which included not only 'two discreet knights' from each county but also two citizens elected by each city and borough. The 1265 Parliament, although summoned primarily to provide support for Simon de Montfort, was the first to include representatives of the towns summoned for a general political purpose. Various other parliaments were held in the next 30 years, usually with no commons in attendance. But a meeting called by Edward I in 1295 to deal with a national emergency brought together all the elements considered capable of giving help, and proved so similar to the broadly national gatherings of later centuries that it has been called the 'Model Parliament'. Those summoned included the lords lay and spiritual, two knights from each county, two citizens from each city and borough, and (for the first time) lesser clergy—making some 400 in all. 'What touches all', the writ of summons said, 'should be approved by all.'

Formation of Two Houses of Parliament

The meetings of the early Parliaments usually took place wherever was convenient to the ruling monarch. When the meeting was in London it was usually opened in the 'Painted Chamber' of the King's palace adjoining the West Minster (that is to say, Westminster Abbey, whose rebuilding had been begun by Edward the Confessor before the Norman Conquest). The monarch sat on the throne at one end, surrounded by the great officers of State and with his tenants-in-chief ranged according to rank on benches at right angles to the throne. The representatives of the commons stood or knelt at the far end. After they had heard the King's requests, the lords and commons withdrew to separate sittings to debate them; they then reassembled in one body to report their decisions through designated spokesmen. (The first reference to a speaker in the Rolls of Parliament is in 1377.)

At the end of the 13th century Parliament consisted of the King, bishops, abbots, temporal peers (earls and barons), representatives of the lower clergy, knights of the counties, citizens and burgesses. By the middle of the 14th century, a significant change in its composition had occurred. The greater barons, bishops and abbots were drawn by community of interests into a single body. The knights regularly met with citizens and burgesses. The minor clergy, finding a more appropriate place in the convocations (ecclesiastical assemblies) of Canterbury and York, dropped out altogether from about 1330. The eventual result was two houses—the House of Lords, consisting of people who attended in response to individual summonses, and the House of Commons, which brought together all members who had been elected in counties, cities and boroughs, and thus attended as representatives.

Increasing Parliamentary Influence

The commons were summoned to Parliament in the first place because the ruling monarchy needed financial aid and, as time went on, they began to realise the strength of their position. By the middle of the 14th century the formula used was in substance the same as that used nowadays in voting supplies to the Crown— that is, money to the Government, namely, 'by the Commons with the advice of the Lords Spiritual and Temporal'. In 1407 Henry IV pledged that henceforth all money grants should be approved by the House of Commons before being considered by the House of Lords.

A similar advance was made in the legislative field. Originally, the King's legislation needed only the assent of his councillors. Starting with the right of individual commoners to present petitions, the Commons as a body gained the right to submit collective petitions. Later, during the 15th century, they gained the right to participate in giving their requests—or 'Bills'—the form of law. The costs of government and war forced the King to turn with increasing frequency to Parliament for supplies. Before supplies were granted he was often called upon, through petitions, to redress stipulated grievances. Since this usually resulted in some kind of legislation, the law-making power, as well as the power to raise taxes, gradually passed into parliamentary hands. The powerful Tudor monarchs made full use of Parliament in securing assent for their domestic and foreign policies.

As its role in government increased, the House of Commons began to claim certain rights and privileges (for example, freedom of speech) from the Sovereign. The Speaker of the House has claimed these privileges on its behalf at the beginning of each Parliament from about the middle of the 16th century, and still claims them today.

The Civil War

The death of Queen Elizabeth and the succession of James VI of Scotland to the English throne in 1603 with the title James I and VI brought about the personal union of the two kingdoms of England and Scotland. In England this launched a new chapter in the parliamentary story. The often arbitrary actions of the first two Stuart kings (James and his son Charles I) led to a struggle between a monarchy believing in its divine right to rule and a Parliament insisting upon its legislative supremacy.

Charles I, who succeeded his father James in 1625, first tried to coerce Parliament and then dispensed with it for 11 years, attempting to provide financial resources for his Government by irregular methods. This failed and he was forced to recall Parliament in 1640. This led to controversies which in two years plunged the country into the armed conflict of the Civil War. At the outset the parliamentary party had no intention of setting up a government by Parliament alone; its object was to force the King to govern according to law. But military successes and changing circumstances led the victorious parliamentarians to conduct political experiments without parallel in British constitutional development.

Following his defeat in battle, Charles was executed in 1649; the monarchy and the House of Lords were abolished; and the country was proclaimed a republic. In 1653 probably the first written constitution in the modern world was put into operation. The republican experiment (which was extended by force of arms to include Scotland) survived for only two years after the death of its dominant figure, the 'Lord Protector', Oliver Cromwell, in 1658. In 1660 the Stuart claimant, having given the guarantees demanded, returned from continental exile and was received with general acclaim as Charles II.

The Revolution of 1688

The restoration of the monarchy left the problem of the relationship between King and Parliament unsolved. During the 25 years of Charles II's reign the problem did not become acute, largely as a result of his political skill. However, within a few months of his death and the accession of his brother James II in 1685, Parliament was prorogued and was not summoned again during the reign. James II's favouritism towards Roman Catholics in an overwhelmingly Protestant country aroused widespread discontent. Parliament was especially offended by the King's attempts to set aside, or suspend, laws which it had passed. In June 1688 a group of leading men invited William, Prince of Orange (and Stadtholder of Holland), a grandson of Charles I and husband of Mary, James II's eldest daughter, to 'bring over an army and secure the infringed liberties' of the country. The result was the 'bloodless revolution' of 1688 — bloodless because James found himself practically without support and fled into exile. Early the following year a 'convention parliament' (so called because it was not summoned in the regular way by a king) declared James to have abdicated and established William and Mary on the throne as joint sovereigns.

The Bill of Rights, 1689

The most significant business of the Parliament of 1689 was to pass the Bill of Rights, which legalised the settlement of the Crown on William and Mary and reaffirmed Parliament's claim to control taxation and legislation.

The Bill laid down the following as 'illegal and pernicious':

—the 'pretended' royal power of suspending or dispensing with laws;

—the levying of taxes without Parliament's assent;

—the arbitrary establishment of royal commissions and courts; and

—the raising or keeping of a standing army in time of peace unless Parliament agreed.

It reaffirmed the right of subjects to petition the King and the right of Members of Parliament to enjoy full freedom of speech and debate. It said that the election of Members of Parliament ought to be free and that Parliaments 'ought to be held frequently'. The main aim of the Bill of Rights was not to alter the constitution, but to list a number of ways in which James II was considered to have abused his powers and to declare these, by Act of Parliament, illegal. In effect, however, the Bill was a landmark in British constitutional development.

Its provisions meant that it was no longer practicable for the Sovereign to ignore the wishes of Parliament, while within

Parliament the wishes of the House of Commons were predominant since that House was the source of financial authority.

The Act of Settlement, 1701

In 1701 it became necessary to preserve the Protestant succession in the probable event of Princess Anne (the second daughter of James II), heir to the throne after the death of William III, having no heir in the direct line to succeed her. The Act of Settlement of 1701 provided that in this event the succession should go to the nearest Protestant representative of the Stuart family—Sophia, Electress of Hanover, a granddaughter of James I, and her heirs; that no person who was a Roman Catholic or who married one should succeed; and that the Sovereign should be a member of the Church of England.

Significance of the Revolution Settlement

The Revolution Settlement as a whole put an end to theories of any rights to the throne independent of the law. It also led to the acceptance of the supremacy of Parliament as the Crown conceded the necessity of parliamentary sanction both for raising taxes and for maintaining a standing army in peace time. (Such permission is still given for only one year at a time.) Administrative functions, however, were left to the Sovereign to exercise with the help of those ministers and other officers he or she chose to appoint, and for some years the ruling monarch remained the centre of executive power. Thus the government of the country at the beginning of the 18th century depended on both the Sovereign and Parliament.

The disadvantage of this situation was that either the Sovereign or Parliament could effectively obstruct the work of the other, if so minded. It therefore became necessary to develop some constitutional convention to prevent this and to enable government to be carried on. A group of ministers, or cabinet, became the link between the executive and the legislative (see pp. 141–4). The ministers were appointed by the Sovereign, but had sufficient supporters in the House of Commons to enable them to persuade Parliament to pass the legislation and vote the taxation which the King's government needed.

Origins of the United Kingdom Parliament

In Scotland it was the religious policy of the Stuarts rather than their methods of government which encountered opposition. Absolutism in secular affairs was accepted and, indeed, welcomed, by the Scottish Parliament during the 17th century. It was primarily for religious reasons that the Scottish people were glad to be rid of James II and VII and accepted William of Orange in his place. But the resultant settlement of the issue of presbyterianism versus episcopalianism made statesmen in Scotland turn their attention to the political relationship between Crown and people, and to claim a measure of responsibility in royal government similar to that attained in England. After a number of proposals and counter-proposals it was agreed in 1705, during the reign of Queen Anne, that it would be to the advantage of each country to become part of a new kingdom of Great Britain under one Crown and with one Parliament. This was an advantage to England because it would have been highly inconvenient (committed as the country then was to wars on the European mainland) to have an independent kingdom on its border. It was also an advantage to Scotland because it needed a proportionate share in overseas trade, from which it would have been excluded as long as it remained a separate country.

The agreed amalgamation took place in 1707. The Treaty for the Union of Scotland and England established a single Parliament for Great Britain: 16 Scottish representative peers took their place in the House of Lords and 45 Scottish members were elected to the House of Commons, raising the total membership of that House to 558. Provision was made for the succession to the Crown in the event of Anne dying without a direct heir in the same terms as had been used, in relation to the Crown of England, in the Act of Settlement in 1701. This provision was embodied in the law of each part of the kingdom and remains part of the constitutional law of the realm.

From 1707 the development of responsibility in government became part of the history, not of England, nor of Scotland, but of Great Britain. The Act for the Union of Great Britain and Ireland 1800 (which abolished the Irish Parliament and gave Ireland representation in Parliament at Westminster) led to the creation of the United Kingdom.

More than 100 years later, the Government of Ireland Act 1920 set up a separate legislature, subordinate to Westminster, for the six counties of Northern Ireland, with powers to deal with internal affairs (see pp. 5–6). The Act also provided for a separate, subordinate legislature for the remaining 26 Irish counties, but this legislature never functioned, and in 1922 the 26 counties left the United Kingdom to become the Irish Free State (now the Irish Republic). As part of the United Kingdom, Northern Ireland sends 17 members to Parliament at Westminster.

Background to the Modern Party System

Parliamentary government based on the party system has been established in Britain only over the past 150 years or so. As recently as the early nineteenth century there was no clear-cut division in the House of Commons along modern party lines. The term 'Whig' and 'Tory' to describe certain political leanings had been in use for about 150 years, but there was virtually no party organisation outside Parliament. The House of Commons consisted not so much of opposing parties as of political groups which could only be classified roughly according to how far they supported or opposed the King's government.

The Extension of the Right to Vote

The reason for this lack of organisation lay, to some extent, in the comparatively small size and exclusive nature of the electorate. In the counties there was a uniform franchise qualification of a freehold (that is, income) of 40 shillings a year, fixed in the 15th century. In the boroughs the franchise varied enormously. In some all adult men or all ratepayers could vote, in some the mayor and corporation elected the Members of Parliament and in others the franchise was restricted to the owners of certain plots of land (burgages). The new industrial areas, such as Manchester (with a population of 133,000), were unrepresented in the Commons while ancient boroughs which had decayed over the years, such as Old Sarum (the original, long deserted site of Salisbury), with no inhabitants, sent two members. Some seats were in the gift of the Government; still more were in the hands of private proprietors. The outcome of elections was decided by a small number of influential citizens, and not by the public at large. The personal influence of a candidate counted for more than the policy of a party; and once an MP had been elected he was under no obligation to follow a party line. In 1830 the total electorate of Britain was only about 500,000 out of an adult population of 10 million.

The first parliamentary Reform Act, in 1832, did not greatly increase the electorate (this rose to only some 720,000 by its provisions), but it put the franchise on a more consistent basis. Perhaps more importantly, it began the process of re-distributing seats in proportion to population. An Act of 1867 in effect enfranchised the urban workers, and another in 1884 the rural workers, extending the vote to most adult males. Female suffrage followed in the twentieth century—first, in 1918, for women aged 30 and over and then, in 1928, for women on the basis of equality with men: the right to vote at the age of 21 years and over. The voting age for both men and women was lowered to 18 in 1969. Of equal importance with these measures to increase the franchise was legislation to ensure that the franchise was exercised freely (the Ballot Act 1872 provided for voting by secret ballot) and was not open to corruption (the Corrupt and Illegal Practices Act 1883).

The expansion of the electorate was accompanied by the organisation of political parties in the modern sense. As the representatives of millions of newly enfranchised men (and later, women), politicians, who had hitherto stood in their constituencies as individuals, began to form coherent parties. These promised to carry out a definite policy based on stated principles which their followers were prepared to support. Alongside party organisation inside the House of Commons came the development of national party organisations outside Parliament—Liberal (formerly called Whig), Conservative (or Tory) and, from the early 20th century, Labour (or Socialist). The comparatively small number of parties has usually produced stable government without sacrificing responsibility.

Since 1911 members of the House of Commons have been paid a salary for their parliamentary work (see p. 34).

The Speaker

The 19th century saw the organisation of the House of Commons on a predominantly party basis; it also saw the impartial role of the Speaker firmly established.

In the Middle Ages the Speaker of the House of Commons at Westminster was more the Sovereign's agent for 'managing' the Commons than an impartial arbiter of the proceedings of the House. During the constitutional struggles of the 17th century the Speaker's role was in a state of flux: Charles I regarded the Speaker as his agent and the Commons regarded him as their representative spokesman. After the events of the late 17th century (see pp. 16-17) the Speaker ceased to be dependent on the Sovereign, and slowly the idea gained ground that, although a member of a political party before election, he should sever all connections with the party after election. The growing recognition, since the latter half of the 19th century, that the basic principle of the party system as it operates in the modern House of Commons can be maintained only if the Speaker exercises his or her function of controlling the House with due impartiality has meant that the Speaker's political neutrality has become traditional in that House.

Membership and Powers of the House of Lords

The basic membership of the House of Lords in England has always been Lords Spiritual and Lords Temporal. Until the Reformation in the 16th century the spiritual peers (arch-bishops, bishops and mitred abbots) were in the majority. With the dissolution of the monasteries the abbots ceased to form part of the upper House and lay peers became predominant. The number of lay peers (that is, holders of peerages created by the monarch) continued to increase and spiritual peers were eventually limited to the present number of 26. In the earliest period of parliamentary history the Sovereign could summon whom he wished to his council, though he always summoned the earls and the more important members of the 'baronage' when they were available. In the 15th century, however, lay membership of the Lords became largely confined to hereditary male peers with a permanent right of summons. (Peeresses in their own right were ineligible for a writ of summons.) Parliamentary union with Scotland in 1707 brought 16 representative Scottish peers (elected by the Scottish peers at the beginning of each Parliament) into the Lords and parliamentary union with Ireland in 1801 brought in representative Irish peers elected by their fellows for life.[7]

Under the Appellate Jurisdiction Act 1876 Lords of Appeal in Ordinary with non-hereditary 'life' peerages were to sit in the House of Lords to assist the House in carrying out its judicial duties. Proposals to create life peers in addition to the law lords were put forward at various times. In 1958 the Life Peerages Act provided for the appointment of life peers and peeresses—giving women, for the first time, the right to sit and vote in the House of Lords.

In 1963 further changes in the composition of the House were effected by the Peerage Act, which gave peers the right to disclaim peerages for their lifetime and so renounce for themselves, but not for their successors, their rights and privileges (and at the same time remove their disqualifications to sit in the House of Commons and to vote at parliamentary elections). The Act also gave peeresses in their own right the same position as hereditary peers for

[7]After the creation of the Irish Free State (now the Irish Republic) the election of Irish peers lapsed; by 1962 there were no representative Irish peers left in the House of Lords.

parliamentary purposes, and gave full rights of admission to all peers and peeresses of Scotland, thus bringing to an end the system of representative peers (see p. 27).

Since the end of the 18th century, when numerous peerages were conferred on the advice of William Pitt the Younger (Prime Minister 1783–1801 and 1804–06), an increasing majority of hereditary peers have been Conservative in sympathy. With the development in the 19th century of the modern party system and of a responsible government dependent on a majority in the elected House of Commons, difficulties of co-operation between the two Houses were sometimes experienced. This was especially the case when a non-Conservative government was in office. Until 1911 the House of Lords had the same legislative powers as the Commons, although for several centuries taxation had been regarded as the preserve of the Commons. The rejection by the Lords of the Liberal government's Budget of 1909 led to a crisis which ended in legislation defining the relations between the two Houses and limiting the delaying powers of the Lords (see p. 26).

Although since 1911 two measures—the Life Peerages Act and the Peerage Act—have affected the structure of the House, no statute has been passed to change its rights and duties, apart from the Parliament Act 1949, which further curtailed its power to delay legislation.

Proposals for fundamental change have been made from time to time and have sometimes reached an advanced stage in discussion, but up to the present no action has been taken.

The Composition of Parliament

British parliamentary government is based on a two-chamber system. The House of Lords (the upper House) and the House of Commons (the lower House) sit separately and are constituted on entirely different principles, but the process of legislation involves both Houses.

Since medieval times the balance of power between the two Houses has undergone a complete change. The continuous process of development has been greatly accelerated during the past 80 years or so. Today the centre of parliamentary power is the popularly elected House of Commons, but until the 20th century the Lords' power of veto over measures proposed by the Commons was, in theory, unlimited. The Parliament Act 1911 imposed restrictions on the Lords' right to delay Bills dealing exclusively with expenditure or taxation and limited their power over other legislation to delaying Bills for two years. This was reduced to one year by the Parliament Act 1949.

These limitations to the powers of the House of Lords are based on the belief that the principal legislative function of the modern House of Lords is revision and that its object is to complement the House of Commons and not to rival it.

The House of Lords

Membership

The House of Lords consists of:

(a) The Lords spiritual: the Archbishops of Canterbury and York, the Bishops of London, Durham and Winchester, and the 21 next most senior diocesan bishops of the Church of England.

(b) The Lords Temporal

—All hereditary peers and peeresses of England, Scotland, Great Britain and the United Kingdom (but not peers of Ireland)

—life peers under the Appellate Jurisdiction Acts 1876 and 1887 to assist the House in its judicial duties (Lords of Appeal or 'law lords'—see pp. 31-2). Some law lords may already be members of the House and all remain so after their retirement.

—All other life peers.

Holders of hereditary peerages have a right to sit in the House of Lords, provided they establish their claim and are aged 21 years or over. However, anyone succeeding to a peerage may, within 12 months of succession, disclaim that peerage for their life-time under the Peerage Act 1963. Disclaimants lose their right to sit in the House of Lords but gain the right to vote and stand as candidates at parliamentary elections. When a disclaimant dies, the peerage passes on down the family in the usual way.

Temporal peerages (both hereditary and life) are created by the Sovereign on the advice of the Prime Minister.[8] They are usually granted either in recognition of distinguished service in politics or other walks of life, or because one of the political parties wishes to have the recipient in the upper House. The House of Lords also

---

[8]Some of the appointments under the 1958 Act are recommended by the Prime Minister after consultation with the Leader of the Opposition and the leader of the Liberal Democrats. In early April 1994 there were 1,202 members of the House, including the two archbishops and 24 bishops. The Lords Temporal consisted of 759 hereditary peers who had succeeded to their titles, 15 hereditary peers who had had their titles conferred on them (including the Prince of Wales), and 402 life peers, of whom 21 were 'Law Lords'.

provides a place in Parliament for people who offer useful advice, but who do not wish to be involved in party politics. Unlike the House of Commons, there is no fixed number of members in the House of Lords. Relatively few are full-time politicians.

Attendance

During the session, the House of Lords meets on Tuesdays and Wednesdays at 14.30 and on Thursdays at 15.00 hours and on most Mondays at 14.30. Friday sittings at 11.00 hours take place when required.

Potential membership of the House is about 1,200 (of whom about 80 are women), but this number is reduced by about 80 by a scheme which allows peers who do not wish to attend to apply for leave of absence for the duration of a Parliament. In addition some hereditary peers do not establish their claim to succeed and so do not receive a writ of summons entitling them to sit in the House; there were around 90 such peers in early 1994. Average daily attendance is about 380, but more peers attend when matters in which they have a special interest are under discussion. During the 1992–93 parliamentary session, 936 peers attended at least once.

Elder statesmen and others who have spent their lives in public service are among the peers who attend the House of Lords most frequently. They receive no salary for their parliamentary work, but may claim for expenses incurred in attending the House (except for judicial sittings)and certain travelling expenses.

The maximum daily rates are as follows:

	£
Overnight subsistence	69
Day subsistence and incidental travel	31
Secretarial costs, postage and certain additional expenses	30

The following may not claim such expenses: the Lord Chancellor, the Chairman of Committees and the Principal Deputy Chairman of Committees, the law lords (all of whom receive salaries) and any member in receipt of a ministerial salary.

Representation of the Government

Most ministers are members of the House of Commons (see p. 35). However, the Government must be fully represented by ministers in the House of Lords as it requires spokesmen and women to put forward its policies in that House.

The House of Lords usually includes about 20 office-holders, among whom are the Government Whips, who are members of the Royal Household,[9] and who act as spokesmen and women for the Government in debate. Their salaries are shown on pp. 37-8. The number of Cabinet ministers in the Lords varies; it is usually between two and four out of a total of over 20.

Officers of the House

Both Houses of Parliament have some members with special functions concerned with the management of business. The House is presided over by the Lord Chancellor,[10] who takes his place on the Woolsack[11] as ex officio Speaker of the House of Lords. The Lord Chancellor is recommended for appointment by the Prime Minister, who is not required to consult the House. As Speaker, the

[9]The Chief Whip on the government side usually holds office as Captain of the Honourable Corps of the Gentlemen at Arms, and his deputy as Captain of the Yeomen of the Guard.

[10]The Lord Chancellor, a Cabinet minister, is also head of the judiciary.

[11]The Woolsack is the traditional name given to the large cushion stuffed with wool, in front of the throne. It was originally made from the wool of English sheep when this was a leading commodity in the country's economy; it presumably symbolised prosperity. The date of its introduction is uncertain. The modern Woolsack is filled, for symbolic reasons, with wool from several countries of the Commonwealth.

Lord Chancellor has very limited powers compared with the Speaker in the House of Commons (see p. 35); the House of Lords decides upon its own procedure and matters of order. On the other hand, as an important member of the Government, with a seat in the Cabinet, the Lord Chancellor often takes an active part in debates, speaking and voting as a member of his or her party. If the Lord Chancellor wishes to address the House in any capacity except that of Speaker, he steps aside from the Woolsack.

In the Lord Chancellor's absence, his place may be taken by a deputy speaker appointed by the Crown or a deputy chairman appointed by the House. The first of the deputy speakers is the Chairman of Committees,[12] who is appointed by the House at the beginning of each session and normally chairs most committees. The Chairman also has general supervision over private Bill legislation (see p. 73), assisted by the Chairman of Committees' Counsel, a permanent salaried officer of the House. The Chairman of Committees does not usually take part in debate on ordinary topics except when presenting the report of a select committee. The Chairman and the Principal Deputy Chairman of Committees are the only Lords who receive salaries as officers of the House (see p. 38).

Other permanent officers of the House of Lords include the Clerk of the Parliaments, who is appointed by the Crown and is responsible for the records of proceedings, including Judgments, Minutes and Journals of the House, and for the text of Acts of Parliament when they have received the Royal Assent. The Clerk also advises on procedure, is Accounting Officer for the cost of the

[12]The appointment of the Chairman of Committees and the Principal Deputy Chairman is for one session only, but in practice, since their work is highly technical and has little to do with party politics, they remain in office until they choose to resign.

House, and is Registrar of the Court for the judicial business of the House.

The Clerk of the Parliaments is in charge of the administrative staff of the House, known collectively as the Parliament Office. This includes the Clerk Assistant, Reading Clerk and Fourth Clerk Judicial. These clerks, who are supported by other clerks and administrative and specialist staff, are appointed by the Lord Chancellor, subject to the formal approval of the House. The Record Office of the House is responsible for the records of the Commons as well as of the Lords.

The Gentleman Usher of the Black Rod, usually known as 'Black Rod', is appointed by the Sovereign and is also Serjeant-at-Arms in attendance upon the Lord Chancellor. The appointment is traditionally given to a former senior officer of the armed forces. As holder of the traditional office of 'Keeper of the Doors', he is in charge of the Doorkeepers and is responsible for security and for admitting strangers to the precincts, whether or not the House is sitting. He is responsible to the Administration and Works Sub-Committees of the Offices Committee for accommodation and services in the House of Lords' part of the Palace of Westminster and also, as secretary to the Lord Great Chamberlain, is responsible for certain ceremonial duties. Black Rod is assisted by the Yeoman Usher, who is also Deputy Serjeant-at-Arms.

Final Court of Appeal

In addition to its parliamentary work, the House of Lords has important legal functions, as the final court of appeal for civil cases in the whole of Britain, and for criminal cases in England, Wales and Northern Ireland. Well over 100 new appeals are presented each year. In theory all Lords are entitled to attend the House when it is sitting as a court of appeal. In practice, by established tradition, judicial business is conducted by

—the Lord Chancellor, who sits from time to time;

—the Lords of Appeal in Ordinary (who are appointed to hear appeals to the House, and are salaried); and—when required—

—other Lords who hold or have held high judicial office.

The House of Commons

The House of Commons is a representative assembly elected by universal adult suffrage, and consists of men and women (Members of Parliament 'MPs') from all sections of the community, regardless of income or occupation. There are 651 seats in the House of Commons: 524 for England, 38 for Wales, 72 for Scotland and 17 for Northern Ireland. Of the 651 MPs, there are at present 59 women, three Asian and three black MPs.

Members of the Commons hold their seats for the lifetime of a Parliament. They are elected either at a general election, which takes place after a Parliament has been dissolved and a new one summoned by the Sovereign, or at a by-election, held when a vacancy occurs in the House as a result of the death or resignation of an MP or as a result of elevation to the House of Lords.

An MP who wishes to resign from the House of Commons can do so only by using the technical device of applying to the Chancellor of the Exchequer for 'an office of profit under the Crown'. The holding of such office is a disqualification for membership of the Commons, and when an MP is appointed to one of these offices, his or her seat is automatically vacated. The two appointments used for this purpose are Crown Steward or Bailiff of the Chiltern Hundreds and Steward of the Manor of Northstead, ancient offices which carry no salary and have no responsibilities. The appointment lasts only until another MP asks for it. A request for appointment is never refused.

Attendance

The House of Commons meets in Westminster from Mondays to Fridays throughout the year, except when Parliament is in recess. The hours of sitting for normal business are: Mondays to Thursdays from 14.30 to 22.30, and Fridays 09.30 to 15.00. Certain business is exempt from normal closing times and other business may be exempted if the House chooses, so that the Commons very often sits later than 22.30 on the first four days of the week. All-night sittings are not uncommon. The House has frequently considered changing the hours at which it meets. There has been some support for the idea of sitting earlier in the day but so far no permanent changes have been made.

MPs, who also have much committee, party and constituency business to attend to, are not normally expected to be present all the time in the debating chamber. When any special business is about to take place for instance, a vote on some legislative or other matter, steps are taken to summon them. At other times, the number of members present varies depending on the speakers and the subject for debate. Some MPs leave the House altogether for a few hours, but the majority remain within the Palace of Westminster so that they can reach the voting lobbies within a few minutes of being called.

In the past, MPs wishing to be away from the House for a period of days during the session had to apply for 'leave of absence'. This is not now considered necessary, but may be granted formally to an official delegation from the House.

Ministers in the Commons

The law regarding the number of ministers who may sit in the House of Commons is based on the Ministers of the Crown Act 1975 and the House of Commons Disqualification Act 1975. A maximum of 95 people holding ministerial office are entitled to sit and vote in the Commons at any one time. This does not include ministers' parliamentary private secretaries (MPs who do not receive any additional official salary).

Payment of MPs

Members of the House of Commons are paid a basic annual salary of £31,687 (from January 1994—see below). This is intended to enable them 'efficiently to discharge the duties of the service, without undue financial worry and to live and maintain themselves and their families at a modest, but honourable level'.[13] This income is subject to income tax, with allowances for expenses in accordance with the general law and practice of taxation.

For some years MPs' salaries, have been related to those paid to civil servants. In 1987 it was agreed that MPs should be paid at a rate of 89 per cent of the maximum point on the salary scale of civil servants on Grade 6 of the Civil Service pay scale (excluding performance related pay). Although this link has been ended by changes in the Civil Service pay system, pay increases for MPs are generally in line with the level so established.

Pensions are regulated by the Parliamentary and Other Pensions Acts 1972–78, which provide for a compulsory contributory scheme to pay pensions to MPs after four years' service on retirement from the House if they have reached the age of 65.

[13]*Report of the Committee on the Remuneration of Ministers and Members of Parliament* (Cmnd 2516), 1964.

Provision is also made for widows' and orphans' benefits. A severance allowance is payable to MPs who either fail to be re-elected at the general election following dissolution, or do not stand for election because their constituencies have ceased to exist due to boundary changes. Grants range from six months' salary for those aged under 50, to up to one year's salary for older or longer serving members. Members are entitled to an office costs allowance of £40,380 for secretarial and research assistance expenses. They also have a number of other allowances:

—inner London members receive a supplement of £1,222 a year; and

—additional costs of other members related to living away from home, up to a maximum of £10,958 in a full year, are reimbursed, based on the existing subsistence rate for the Civil Service.

MPs are also entitled to free stationery, postage and inland telephone calls from within the House of Commons, and to travel or car mileage allowances.

Ministers in the Commons receive, in addition to their ministerial salaries, a reduced parliamentary salary of £23,854 a year in recognition of their constituency responsibilities, as distinct from their ministerial or other responsibilities. They are entitled to claim the other allowances paid to members of the House.

The salaries for ministers, the Leader of the Opposition in the House of Commons and House of Lords, together with the Whips in both Houses,[14] and for Members of Parliament, including the Speaker and his deputies in the Commons, are shown on pp. 37-8.

[14]In the House of Lords both the Government Chief Whip and the Deputy Chief Whip receive salaries for their duties as members of the Royal Household (see pp. 37-8).

Officers of the House

The chief officer of the House of Commons is the Speaker. This office has been held continuously since 1377, and its powers have been exercised with complete impartiality since at least the middle of the 19th century.

The Speaker has two main functions: first, he or she is the representative of the House in its relations with the Crown, the House of Lords and other authorities; second, he or she presides over the House and enforces the observance of all rules which govern its conduct.

The quality most essential to Speakers is strict impartiality, and one of their most important duties is to protect the rights of minorities and to ensure that their voices are heard. All members look to the Speaker for guidance in matters of procedure, and he or she decides points of order and gives rulings when required. The Speaker must be seen to be above party political controversy in all matters. Even after Speakers retire, they take no part in political issues. Speakers must keep themselves apart from their former party colleagues or any one group or interest. They do not, for instance, eat in the Commons dining room, and do not attend meetings of parties or other interest groups.

The Commons elects its own Speaker—the usual practice is for the Government, after consultation with the Opposition, to put forward the name of an MP acceptable to all sections of the House, who is then proposed and seconded by members of the backbenches. It has become a generally accepted principle that, once the Speaker has been elected in one Parliament, he or she is re-elected in subsequent Parliaments, and thus remains in office until he or she chooses to retire (or dies). The Speaker continues as an MP, dealing like any other with constituents' letters and problems, but neither speaks nor votes in the House. (In the event of a tie, however, see p. 61.) When seeking re-election at the national polls, the Speaker remains aloof from party issues—standing as 'the Speaker seeking re-election'.

The Speaker also has a number of duties concerning the functions of the House and is in control of the Commons part of the Palace of Westminster and its precincts. Control of Westminster Hall and the Crypt Chapel is vested jointly in the Lord Great Chamberlain (representing the Sovereign), the Lord Chancellor, and the Speaker.

The Speaker has a residence within the Palace of Westminster. On retirement, the Speaker is offered a peerage and is provided with a pension.

Other Officers

Other parliamentary officers of the House are the Chairman of Ways and Means and two Deputy Chairmen, all of whom may act as deputy Speaker. These officers are elected by the House on the nomination of the Government and, like the Speaker, they neither speak nor vote in the House other than in their official capacity. They also receive the reduced parliamentary salary of £23,854 in addition to their ministerial salaries.

Table 1: Ministerial and Other Salaries[a]

	Salary (including parliamentary salary) from January 1994
Prime Minister	78,292
Cabinet Minister (Commons)	64,739
Cabinet Minister (Lords)	52,260
Minister of State (Commons)	52,790
Minister of State (Lords)	46,333
Parliamentary Under Secretary (Commons)	45,815
Parliamentary Under Secretary (Lords)	38,894
Attorney General	67,310
Solicitor General	59,486
Lord Advocate	52,340
Solicitor General for Scotland[b]	45,539
House of Commons	
Leader of the Opposition	61,349
Chief Whip	57,891
Deputy Chief Whip	52,790
Opposition Chief Whip	52,790
Government Whip	42,474
Assistant Opposition Whip	42,474
Chairman of Ways and Means	52,790
Deputy Chairman of Ways and Means	49,285
The Speaker[c]	66,763
Member of Parliament	31,687
House of Lords[d]	
Chief Whip	46,333
Deputy Chief Whip	38,894

Table 1: Ministerial and Other Salaries[a] *continued*

	Salary (including parliamentary salary) from January 1994
Government Whip	35,099
Leader of the Opposition	38,894
Opposition Chief Whip	35,099
Chairman of Committees	46,333
Principal Deputy Chairman of Committees	42,354

[a]Figures for members of the Commons include a proportion of parliamentary salary of £23,854 a year.

[b]The Solicitor General for Scotland's salary has been adjusted because the holder of the office is in neither House.

[c]The present Speaker has chosen to take the same salary as a Commons' Cabinet minister.

[d]The Lord Chancellor's salary is set separately by the Ministerial and Other Pernsions and Salaries Act 1991; he currently receives £120,179.

Departments of the House

The House of Commons has six administrative and executive departments:

—the Department of the Clerk of the House;

—the Department of the Serjeant-at-Arms;

—the Department of the Library;

—the Department of the Official Report of the House of Commons;

—the Administration Department; and

—the Refreshment Department.

Of the permanent officers of the House[15] (who are not MPs), the most important is the Clerk of the House of Commons, appointed by the Crown. The Clerk conducts the business of the House in the department under his or her control and is the principal adviser to the Speaker and MPs on the law, practice and procedures of Parliament. He or she is also the Accounting Officer for the House of Commons vote and head of the Clerk's Department (see below). The Clerk Assistant, who is also appointed by the Crown, sits at the Table of the House, together with the Clerk of the House. The Clerk of Committees oversees all official committees of the House and is appointed by the Clerk of the House.

The Clerk's Department advises the Speaker and MPs (including ministers) on the practice and procedure of the House. Its services are concerned with proceedings in the House itself, with the legislative process, with select committees and with overseas Parliaments, both Commonwealth and foreign, and international parliamentary assemblies. The Vote Office provides the documentation required for proceedings in the House and its committees, for the individual needs of members and for officers of the House.

The Serjeant-at-Arms, who is appointed by the Sovereign, waits upon the Speaker with the Mace (the symbol of the royal authority by which the House meets), and carries out certain orders of the House. He or she is the official housekeeper of the Commons part of the building and is generally responsible for its security. The Department of the Serjeant-at-Arms deals with order and security in the precincts of the House and ceremonial, communications, and accommodation matters, and is responsible for the work of the Parliamentary Works Directorate for the Palace of Westminster (see p. 41).

[15]For full list, see Appendix 3.

The Department of the Library provides MPs with information required in connection with their parliamentary duties. As well as books and documents, it provides written answers to enquiries from MPs involving research, detailed background analyses, abstracts and bibliographies, and sometimes helps to service select committees. The general library provides an information service, for members and their staff, and provides the computer information system POLIS (Parliamentary On-Line Information Service), which gives access to a wide range of parliamentary information. The Public Information Office of the House of Commons is administered by the Department of the Library.

The Department of the Official Report is responsible for reporting all the sittings of the House and of its standing committees, and producing the Official Report (*Hansard*, see p. 65).

The Administration Department consists of the Fees Office, which deals with pay and allowances for MPs and staff, the Establishments Office, which deals with staff matters for the whole House of Commons; and the Computer Office, whose staff act for both Houses.

The Refreshment Department provides eating and drinking facilities for members and staff of the House. Service is available whenever the House is sitting, however late that might be.

Within the administrative departments of the House of Commons there are nearly 1,030 full-time and 60 part-time staff. The departments are under the supervision of the House of Commons Commission, a statutory body composed of MPs, and chaired ex officio by the Speaker.

The Parliamentary Works Directorate (part of the Serjeant-at-Arms Department), under the control of both Houses, is responsible for the fabric of the Palace and the provision of furnishing, fuel and lighting.

'Allied' Services

Some services are not performed by departments of the House. It pays for services provided by HMSO (Her Majesty's Stationery Office), telecommunications operators, the Post Office and the Metropolitan Police.

Stationery and printing are provided on repayment by HMSO; and the Post Office covers postal services. The Metropolitan Police make available (on repayment) police officers for regular duty, and provide extra police as needed (for instance, to cope with mass lobbying).

Parliamentary Elections

Constituencies

For electoral purposes, Britain is divided into geographical areas known as constituencies, each returning one member to the House of Commons. To ensure that constituency electorates are kept roughly equal, four Parliamentary Boundary Commissions—one each for England, Scotland, Wales and Northern Ireland—carry out reviews of parliamentary and European Parliamentary constituencies every 10 to 15 years. They recommend any adjustment of seats that may seem necessary in the light of population movements or other changes.

A commission may also submit interim reports on particular constituencies if, for instance, it is necessary to bring constituency boundaries into line with altered local government boundaries. The last general reports of the Commissions for England, Wales and Scotland were approved by Parliament in 1983, and that for Northern Ireland in 1982.[16] In 1993 the average number of electors for each constituency was about 69,500 in England; 58,500 in Wales; 54,600 in Scotland; and 67,800 in Northern Ireland. There are at present 651 constituencies.

Voters

The law relating to parliamentary elections is largely set out in the Representation of the People Acts 1983 and 1985. Under their pro-

[16]For further information on elections, see *Parliamentary Elections* (Aspects of Britain: HMSO, 1991).

visions election to the House of Commons is decided by secret ballot. British citizens, together with citizens of other Commonwealth countries and citizens of the Irish Republic resident in Britain may vote provided they are aged 18 or over and not legally disqualified from voting.[17] To be entitled to vote in a constituency electors have to be registered in the current electoral register for that constituency. The electoral register for each constituency is prepared annually by electoral registration officers. 'Service' voters (members of the armed forces, Crown servants such as embassy or consular officials, and staff of the British Council who are employed overseas, together with their wives or husbands, if accompanying them) may be registered for an address in a constituency where they would live but for their service. The Representation of the People Act 1989 extended the right to vote to British citizens living abroad by increasing from 5 to 20 years the period during which they may apply to be registered to vote.

Calling a General Election

When a decision has been taken to dissolve Parliament, the following orders are made by the Queen in Council:

—the Lord Chancellor is directed to affix the Great Seal to the royal proclamation for dissolving the old and calling the new Parliament; and

—the Lord Chancellor and Secretary of State for Northern Ireland are directed to issue the Writs of Election.

[17]The following people are not entitled to vote in a parliamentary election: members of the House of Lords; aliens; patients detained under mental health legislation; convicted offenders detained in custody; and anyone convicted within the previous five years of illegal election practices.

The writs are normally issued on the same day as the proclamation summoning the new Parliament.

It is usual for the Prime Minister to announce the dissolution of Parliament and explain the reasons for holding the election. Polling takes place 17 days after the dissolution, not including week-ends, bank holidays and days of public thanksgiving or mourning. General elections are usually held on Thursdays, though this is not required by law.

By-elections

By-elections take place when a parliamentary seat falls vacant between general elections. When a by-election is to be held, the Speaker of the House of Commons issues a warrant to the Clerk of the Crown directing the Clerk to issue a Writ of Election. If a vacancy occurs while Parliament is meeting, the motion for a new writ is normally moved by the party to which the former MP belonged.

Administration of Elections

The Home Office (in England and Wales), the Scottish Home and Health Department and the Northern Ireland Office are responsible for overseeing electoral law. Elections are administered by the returning officer. In practice the duties are carried out by a deputy or acting returning officer (a local government official).

The official expenses of a parliamentary election, as distinct from candidates' expenses (see p. 47), are paid by the Government.

Voting

Voting is not compulsory, but at a general election the majority of the electorate (76.9 per cent of a total of 43.3 million people entitled to vote at the general election in April 1992) exercise their right. At by-elections polling percentages are often much lower. Electors whose circumstances on polling day are such that they cannot reasonably be expected to vote in person at their local polling station—for example, electors away on holiday—may apply for an absent vote at a particular election.

Electors who are physically incapacitated or unable to vote in person because of the nature of their work or because they have moved to a new area, may apply for an indefinite absent vote. People entitled to an absent vote may vote by post or by proxy, but postal ballot papers cannot be sent to addresses outside Britain.

Each constituency is divided into a number of polling districts (wards in Northern Ireland). In each district or ward there is a polling station. Most are in schools, but many other types of building are also used.

The hours of voting are 07.00 to 22.00. Voting takes place in booths which are screened to maintain secrecy. The voter marks the ballot papers with a cross in the box opposite the name of the candidate of his or her choice.

Postal ballot papers, together with a 'declaration of identity', ballot paper envelopes and return postal envelopes are sent to people entitled to vote by post. Votes must reach the returning officer by the close of the poll.

The votes must be counted as soon as practicable after the poll at a place chosen by the returning officer. The returning officer declares the result of the poll, usually in public. Most results are known within five or six hours of the close of poll.

People wishing to question the conduct or result of an election must do so by presenting an election petition which is tried in open court.

Candidates

Any man or woman who is a British citizen, a citizen of another Commonwealth country or a citizen of the Irish Republic, may stand for election provided they are aged 21 or over and are not disqualified. Those disqualified from election include:

—undischarged bankrupts;

—people sentenced to more than one year's imprisonment;

—members of the House of Lords;

—clergy of the Churches of England, Scotland and Ireland and the Roman Catholic Church; and

—those precluded under the House of Commons Disqualification Act 1975. These include holders of judicial office, civil servants, members of the regular armed forces, police officers, and British members of the legislature of any country or territory outside the Commonwealth.

Holders of a wide range of public posts—for instance, in public corporations and government commissions—are also disqualified. Candidates usually belong to one of the main national political parties, although smaller parties or groupings also put forward candidates, and individuals may be nominated without party support.

A candidate's nomination for election must be signed by two electors as proposer and seconder, and by eight other electors registered in the constituency.

Each candidate must also deposit £500 during the period allowed for delivery of nomination papers. If candidates receive at least 5 per cent of the total votes cast their deposit is returned; if not, their deposit is lost. The deposit is intended to ensure that candidates are seriously seeking election.

Each parliamentary candidate appoints an election agent, who is responsible for running the campaign and, in particular, for controlling expenses. All orders for printing and advertising must be given by candidates or their agents.

Election Expenses

Candidates' election expenses are strictly regulated; breaches of the law are punishable by severe penalties. The maximum sum of money a candidate may spend on an election campaign is currently £4,642, plus 3.9 pence for each elector in borough constituencies and 5.2 pence for each elector in county constituencies. (County constituencies normally cover large rural areas, and expenses are thus greater than in the smaller, mainly urban, borough constituencies.) In a constituency of 60,000 electors, therefore, the total permissible expenses are £6,982 in a borough constituency, and £7,762 in a county constituency. The prescribed scale is not required to cover the candidate's personal expenses, for instance, the cost of living at a hotel during the election campaign but any such expenses beyond £600 must be paid by the candidate's election agent and accounted for in his or her return of election expenses. A candidate may post free of charge an election address to each elector in the constituency.

By-election Expenses

Under the Representation of the People Act 1989 separate, higher limits have been set for spending in by-election campaigns. The maximum amount which may be spent is £18,572 plus 15.8 pence for each elector in borough constituencies and £18,572 plus 20.8 pence for each elector in county constituencies. These limits are intended to reflect the fact that by-elections in individual constituencies are often regarded as tests of national opinion in the period between general elections. The limits on candidates' expenditure do not apply to the amounts that may be spent by national party organisations on campaigning. They may spend what they like on party political broadcasts, transport for party leaders and general publicity.

Corrupt and Illegal Practices

Certain offences connected with elections committed by candidates or their agents, or with their knowledge and consent, make a candidate's election invalid (or void).

Broadcasting

Arrangements for party election broadcasts on radio and television during general elections are made by a committee consisting of representatives of the political parties, the BBC (British Broadcasting Corporation), the ITC (Independent Television Commission) and the Radio Authority. Party election broadcasts are transmitted on the BBC 1, BBC 2 and independent television channels. The amount of time each party is allowed depends in part on the number of candidates it has in the election and its strength in the previous Parliament.

System of Voting

The system of voting used is the simple majority system: candidates are elected if they have a majority of votes over the next candidate, although not necessarily a majority over the sum of the other candidates' votes.

Speaker's Conference

Questions concerning changes in electoral law are considered peri-odically at a Speaker's Conference, consisting of MPs meeting under the chairmanship of the Speaker. As with other parliamen-tary committees, party representation at the Conference reflects that of the House. The proceedings are in private and recommen-dations are published in the form of letters from the Speaker to the Prime Minister. Five such conferences have been held this century, the last in 1978.

The Party System

The existence of organised political parties which lay their own policies before the electorate has led to well-developed political divisions in Parliament. These are considered to be vital to democratic government.[18] The party system has existed in one form or another since at least the 18th century, and began to assume its modern shape towards the end of the 19th century. Whenever there is a general election (or a by-election) the parties may put up candidates for election; other people may also stand. The electorate then decides, by voting for candidates at the polls on election day, which of the opposing policies it would like to see put into effect. The candidate who polls the most votes is elected; an absolute majority is not required.

Since 1945 eight general elections have been won by the Conservative Party and six by the Labour Party; the great majority of members of the House of Commons have represented either one or other of these two parties. Since an MP represents, on average, some 67,000 electors, in nearly all cases election depends on the work of a large-scale organisation. Although candidates outside the main parties may be, and have been, elected, this tends to be an exception.[19] See Appendix 1 for details of the results of the last general election.

---

[18]See *Organisation of Political Parties* (Aspects of Britain: HMSO, 1994).
[19]There is at present one MP, Sir James Kilfedder, the Ulster Popular Unionist MP for Down North, who was elected without the support of a party machine.

Government and Opposition

The party which wins most seats (but not necessarily the most votes) at a general election, or which has the support of a majority of members in the Commons, is usually invited by the Sovereign to form a Government. If no party wins an overall majority of seats a minority government may be formed.

By tradition, the leader of the majority party is appointed Prime Minister by the Sovereign, and chooses a team of ministers, including a Cabinet of about 20 members. The Prime Minister and other government ministers receive annual salaries from public funds (see p. 37).

The party with the next largest number of seats is officially recognised as 'Her Majesty's Opposition' (or 'the Official Opposition'),[20] with its own leader (who receives a salary in addition to a parliamentary salary—see p. 38) and its own 'shadow cabinet', whose members speak on the subjects for which government ministers have responsibility. The Leader of the Opposition has no official function according to legislation or parliamentary rules. However, in practice he or she, through control of the Opposition Whips, plays a large part in deciding, with the Government, the business arrangements of the House of Commons (see p. 54). Members of any other parties and any independent MPs who have been elected support or oppose the Government according to their party or their own views. Opposition parties are also represented in the House of Lords.

The Government is primarily responsible for arranging the business of the two Houses. As the initiator of policy, it indicates

[20]The term 'His Majesty's Opposition' was first used in the early 19th century. However the concept of parliamentary opposition is older; the phrase 'opposition bench' was, for example, in current use by 1770.

which action it wishes Parliament to take, and explains and defends its position in public debate. Governments of the past were frequently obliged by members of their own party to withdraw measures. Today most governments can usually count on the voting strength of their supporters in the Commons and, depending on the size of their overall majority, can thus ensure that their legislation is passed in substantially the form that they originally proposed. This development, which is the result of the growth of party discipline, has strengthened the hand of the Government, but it has also increased the importance of the Opposition.

The greater part of the work of exerting pressure through criticism now falls on the Opposition, which is expected and given the opportunity, according to the practice of both Houses, to develop its own position in Parliament and state its own views. In general its aims are to contribute to the formulation of policy and legislation by constructive criticism; to oppose government proposals it considers objectionable; to seek amendments to government Bills; and to put forward its own policies in order to improve its chances of winning at the next general election. Opposition parties are also represented on standing and select committees in proportion to their strength in the Commons. The chairmen or women of some of the select committees are drawn from the official Opposition party.

Seating of Members

Seating arrangements in both Houses of Parliament reflect the nature of the party system (see pp. 121 and 123). Both debating chambers are rectangular in shape, are overlooked by galleries, and have at one end the seat of the Speaker and at the other end a formal barrier, known as the 'Bar'. The benches for members run the length of the chamber, on both sides. The benches to the right of the Speaker are used by the Government and its supporters; those to the left are occupied by the Opposition and members of any other parties. (When the Government has a very large majority, some of its supporters may sit on the Opposition side of the Chamber.) In the House of Lords, there are also the bishops' benches and a number of cross-benches for peers who do not wish to attach themselves to any party.

Leaders of the Government and of the Opposition sit on the front benches of their respective sides with their supporters (the backbenchers) sitting behind them. In the House of Commons, where there is room for only 346 MPs on the benches, back-benchers may also sit in the side galleries, which can accommodate a further 91 members. In both Houses the galleries also provide accommodation for visitors, diplomats, the Press and government and parliamentary officials.

Leader of the House of Commons

The Leader of the House of Commons is the government minister with primary responsibility for organising the business of the House, and for providing reasonable facilities for the House to debate matters about which it is concerned. One of the Leader's functions is to announce the following week's programme to the House (after this has been settled by the Chief Whips—see below) in answer to a question from the Opposition (usually at 15.30 hrs on Thursdays). The Leader may also move procedural motions relating to the business of the House.

In the absence of the Prime Minister, the Leader of the House of Commons acts as the spokesman or woman of the Government on ceremonial and other occasions. The Leader of the House of Lords has similar functions in the Lords.

The Whips

Outside Parliament, party business is conducted by national and local organisations. Inside Parliament, it is conducted by officers known as Whips,[21] who are MPs and peers (chosen within their parliamentary party). Their duties include:

—keeping members informed of forthcoming parliamentary business;

—maintaining the party's voting strength by ensuring members attend important debates and support their party in divisions (the taking of votes); and

—passing on to the party leadership the opinions of backbench members.

The term 'whip' also applies to the weekly circular letter sent out by each Chief Whip to all members within the same party requesting their attendance at particular times and notifying them of parliamentary business.

The relative importance a party attaches to attendance for debates and divisions listed in the circular notice is indicated by their being underlined once, twice or three times. Items underlined once are considered routine and attendance is optional; those underlined twice are more important and attendance is required unless (in the Commons) a 'pair'—that is, a member of an opposing party who also intends to be absent from a division—has been arranged; items underlined three times are highly important and

[21]The term 'whip' derives from fox-hunting, where whippers-in or whips are used by a hunt to look after the hounds and prevent them from straying.

pairing is not normally allowed. In the Commons, failure to attend after receiving a 'three-line Whip' is usually seen as rebellion against the party's policy and renders members liable to disciplinary action by their party.

Whips in the House of Lords

The Whips in the Lords are less exclusively concerned with party matters. Party discipline tends to be less strong in the Lords than in the Commons, since Lords have less hope of high office and no need of party support in elections. In the House of Lords there is a Convenor of cross-bench peers, and cross-bench peers may receive an unlined whip which outlines business but does not include any voting or attendance instructions. Pairing does not take place in the Lords.

In the House of Lords both the Government Chief Whip and the Opposition Chief Whip receive a salary from public funds. The Government Chief Whip is assisted by Government Whips who, as in the House of Commons, are paid; the Opposition Whips are not paid.

The Government Whips in the Lords hold offices in the Royal Household; unlike those in the Commons, they also act as government spokesmen and women.

Whips in the House of Commons

In the Commons the party Whips consist of the Chief Whip and, in the two main parties, the Deputy Chief Whip and a varying number of junior Whips, all of whom are MPs. Each of the smaller opposition parties also normally has a Whip. Those of the party in power are known as Government Whips and are paid out of public funds.

The formal title of the Government Chief Whip is Parliamentary Secretary to the Treasury. Of the other Government Whips, three are officers of the Royal Household (one of these is Deputy Chief Whip), five have the title of Lord Commissioner of the Treasury,[22] and five are Assistant Whips. The Opposition Whips have no official position, although the Opposition Chief Whip in both Houses receives a salary, as do two other Opposition Assistant Whips in the Commons. Whips' salaries are in addition to their parliamentary salary.

The Government Chief Whip is directly answerable to the Prime Minister and the Leader of the Commons. Subject to the Cabinet, the overriding responsibility for the organisation of business in the House of Commons and the progress of the Government's legislative programme rests with the Leader of the House. Under the authority of the Leader, the Government Chief Whip in the Commons attends the Cabinet and makes the day-to-day arrangements for the Government's programme of business (estimating the time likely to be needed for each item and discussing the proposed business arrangements with the Opposition). The Chief Whip is also responsible for securing majorities for the Government. He or she is assisted by a small Civil Service staff, headed by the Private Secretary, who is frequently consulted by the Leader of the House.

The Opposition Chief Whip carries out similar duties for his or her own party. The Opposition Chief Whip receives advance notice of the Government's programme each week, and no final decision is taken by the Government until after consultation with the Opposition Chief Whip. The Chief Whips together constitute the 'usual channels' often referred to in the House when the question of finding time for debating a particular issue is discussed.

---

[22]These Junior Lords of the Treasury devote their time to Parliament; their Treasury posts involve little more than signing documents.

The junior Whips are responsible for keeping in touch with individual MPs and conveying their opinions to the Chief Whip. There are about 12 Whips on each side, each responsible for 20 to 30 MPs, usually grouped on a regional basis.

Party Organisations

Conservative Party

The most important organ of the Conservative Party in Parliament is the Conservative and Unionist Members' Committee, commonly known as the 1922 Committee. Named after the year in which it was formed, this Committee normally meets once a week and consists of the backbench membership of the party in the Commons. It is not authorised to decide policy or to control directly the activities of the Party's leader or the front bench. However it serves to represent Conservative opinion in the Commons, and it is upon this Committee's support that the leader's position in the Party depends.

The Committee is independent and has its own organisation; when the party is in office, ministers attend its meetings by invitation and not by right; when the party is in opposition all members of the Party in the Commons may attend meetings. When the Party is in opposition, the leader appoints a consultative committee, which acts as the Party's 'shadow cabinet'. There are no members of the Lords in the 1922 Committee; Conservative peers hold their meetings separately.

Labour Party

The Parliamentary Labour Party (PLP) is composed of all Labour members in both Houses. When the Labour Party is in office, a parliamentary committee acts as a channel of communication between the Government and its backbenchers in both Houses. Half of the committee is elected by the backbench Labour members of the Commons and the remainder are government representatives; these include the Leader of the House, the Government Chief Whip and four others, including a Labour peer, appointed by the party leader. When Labour is in opposition, the PLP is run by an elected parliamentary committee (often referred to as the 'shadow cabinet'). Meetings of the PLP, at which broad outlines of policy are discussed and important decisions sometimes taken, are held at least twice each week. The party leader and his or her colleagues are expected to attend and do so whenever possible, whether the Party is in or out of office. In general, the PLP has a greater measure of influence over policy than its Conservative counterpart.

Liberal Democrats

The Liberal Democrats meet each week to discuss forthcoming parliamentary business and other matters; the leader takes the chair. All MPs and several peers attend.

Party Committees

As well as attending party meetings, both Conservative and Labour MPs have a policy committee system, organised around subject areas which roughly correspond to those of government departments. Both main parties have about 20 groups of this kind, covering, for instance, agriculture and food, defence, finance, trade and industry, education, health, and foreign and Commonwealth affairs. In the Parliamentary Labour Party there are also regional groups. The Liberal Democrats have working parties established by, and reporting to, a standing committee which is responsible for developing party policy.

Parliamentary Procedure

Parliamentary procedure,[23] which includes forms of proceeding, rules of procedure, and recognised parliamentary conventions, is not subject to any comprehensive code. Both Houses have made their own standing and sessional orders,[24] but these are in addition to the unwritten rules of practice which have developed in the course of the transaction of business in each House. Some of the old-established rules of practice were laid down in the 16th century and even earlier; modern practice in the House of Commons often derives from rulings given by Speakers or their deputies.

System of Debate

The system of debate is similar in both Houses: subject starts off as a proposal or 'motion' made by a member. When a motion has been moved, the Speaker proposes the question (in the same terms as the motion) as the subject of debate. After debate, in which each member may speak only once, the question may be decided without voting or by a simple majority vote. The rules governing the contents of speeches and the time and manner of speaking are likewise similar. In both Houses, members speak from wherever they have been sitting and not from a rostrum (although front-bench members

[23]A full description of parliamentary procedure is contained in Erskine May's *Treatise on the Law, Privileges, Proceedings and Usage of Parliament* (see Further Reading, p. 145).
[24]Standing orders are rules which stand until the House amends or revokes them; sessional orders are rules limited to the session in which they are made. In both Houses, certain sessional orders are renewed regularly on the first day of each session.

usually stand at one of the despatch boxes on the Table of the House). They may not read their speeches (although they may refresh their memories by referring to notes which, in the case of ministers, may well be extensive, particularly when explaining the details of government policy). Generally, no member may speak twice to the same motion, except to clarify some part of a speech that has been misunderstood, or 'by leave of the House'.

The Powers of the Speaker

The main difference of procedure between the two Houses lies in the powers of the Chair. In the House of Lords the Speaker or Chairman has no authority to check or curtail debate. Members of the House of Lords do not address themselves to the Speaker during debates, but to all their fellow members in the House. If two peers rise to speak at the same time during a debate, the House itself, not the Speaker, determines who shall speak.

In contrast the Speaker of the House of Commons presides over the House and has full authority to enforce the rules of the House. In debate all speeches are addressed to the Speaker or his or her deputies, and they call upon MPs to speak. If they rise to give a ruling on a doubtful point, or for any other reason, they must be heard in silence, and while they are on their feet no other MP may remain standing. The Speaker must guard against abuse of procedure or any infringement of minority rights, and has discretion to allow or disallow a closure (a motion to end discussion so that the matter may be put to the vote—a function which may also be exercised by the Deputy Speakers). The Speaker and his or her deputies also have certain powers to check irrelevance and repetition in debate, and to save time in other respects. In cases of grave and continuous disorder, they have powers to adjourn the House or suspend the sitting. In cases of wilful disobedience to their instructions by one MP or more, the Speaker or Deputy Speakers can name them, which will result in their suspension—for a period—from the House.

Voting

House of Commons

Voting in the House of Commons takes place under the direction of the Speaker, who announces the final result. In the event of a tied vote, the Speaker gives the casting vote, but without expressing an opinion on the merits of the question and in such a way as to give the House another chance to decide.

A vote is taken by means of a division (that is to say the separation into two lobbies of the MPs who wish to vote for or against a question). MPs voting 'Aye' (yes) go out of the Chamber into the lobby on the right of the Speaker, those voting 'No' pass into the lobby on his or her left. Votes are recorded by four clerks (whose records are later printed in the official Division Lists, and also recorded next day in *Hansard*) and four tellers (two MPs from each side of the House). One teller for the 'ayes' and another for the 'noes' are present in each lobby to check each other in the telling (counting). A division in the Commons may take about ten minutes; there may be two or three hundred divisions in a session.

House of Lords

The voting procedure in the House of Lords is similar to that in the Commons except that the Speaker or Chairman has an ordinary, not a casting, vote. The general principle is that Bills and subordinate legislation may proceed unless a majority votes to reject or amend them. On other motions the question is decided in the negative unless a majority is in favour. When the House is sitting in its judicial role, the judgment under appeal is not changed if the votes are equal.

Disclosure of Financial Interests

House of Commons

The declaration of interests by MPs is governed by two resolutions passed by the House of Commons in 1974. The first stated that in any proceedings of the House or in transactions with other members or with ministers or civil servants, MPs must disclose any relevant financial interest or benefit. The second established a register, open to public inspection, in which MPs would record any relevant interest.

The Register of Members' Interests was first published in 1975. A new Register is compiled at the beginning of each Parliament; it is maintained on a day-to-day basis, and is open to public inspection, and is published once during each session of Parliament. A printed edition is made available for sale annually.

MPs are responsible for what is recorded about themselves. They are obliged to bear in mind the purpose of the Register, which is to provide information of any financial interest or other material benefit which MPs may receive which might be thought to affect their conduct as MPs or influence their actions, speeches or vote in Parliament, and in particular to declare their interests under the following classes:

—Paid directorships of companies, public or private.[25]

—Paid employment or offices.

[25]On assuming office ministers must resign directorships in private and public companies, and must arrange their affairs so that there is no conflict between public duties and private interests.

—Trades, professions or vocations for which MPs are paid.

—The names of clients in cases where MPs' personal services are related to their membership of the House of Commons (this includes, for instance, public relations work, solicitors' work and accountancy).

—Financial sponsorships (a) as a parliamentary candidate where to the knowledge of the MP the sponsorship exceeds a quarter of the candidate's election expenses; or (b) as an MP, by any person or organisation, stating whether any such sponsorship includes payment to the MP or any direct or indirect material advantage.

—Overseas visits relating to membership of the House of Commons, where the cost has not been met wholly by the MP or by public funds.

—Payments or benefits received from overseas governments, organisations or individuals (including payments received by companies in which members have a controlling interest, or the largest shareholding).

—Land and property of substantial value or from which substantial income is derived.

—The names of companies or other bodies in which MPs have, to their knowledge, either themselves or on behalf of their spouse or infant children, a beneficial interest in shareholdings of a nominal value greater than 1 per cent of the issued share capital.

An MP who has a financial interest in a matter before the House of Commons which is direct, immediate and personal, and not held in common with the rest of the country's citizens, is not allowed to vote on it. In practice, however, circumstances rarely arise where an MP is not free to vote. Members' personal staff and lobby journalists working in the House must also declare their interests.

House of Lords

There is no register of financial interests in the House of Lords. Instead there is a long-standing custom that members always speak on their personal honour. Lords therefore decide for themselves whether it is proper to take part in any debate or vote. If they decide to speak on a subject in which they have a direct financial interest, they are expected to declare it. A member also generally declares any further interest which the House should know about in order to form a balanced judgement on his or her speech. Lords are expected not to promote or oppose in the House any Bill or subordinate legislation for which they have received any financial reward.

Quorum of the House

In the House of Commons there is no requirement that a certain number of MPs be present for business to be transacted. If, however, fewer than 40 MPs take part in a division, the business under consideration is held over until the next sitting of the House and the next item of business is taken. The quorum in the House of Lords is three, but if, on questions relating to Bills and delegated legislation, fewer than 30 Lords vote, the Speaker or chairman declares that the question has not been decided and the debate is adjourned to a subsequent sitting.

Publication of Proceedings

Proceedings of both Houses of Parliament are public, except on extremely rare occasions. The minutes (in the House of Commons called Votes and Proceedings and in the Lords Minutes of Proceedings) and the speeches, including those made in second reading committees and standing committees (The Official Report of Parliamentary Debates, *Hansard*), are published daily (see p. 40).

The Law-making Process

The law undergoes constant reform in the courts as established principles are interpreted, clarified or reapplied to meet new circumstances. Fundamental changes are the responsibility of Parliament and the Government through the normal legislative process.

All laws must be approved by the Queen in Parliament. A draft law takes the form of a parliamentary Bill, must go through the necessary stages in both Houses of Parliament and the Queen must signify her approval (which is a formality), all within a single session of Parliament. The Bill then becomes an Act and comes into force on the day on which it receives the Royal Assent, unless the Act provides for other dates.

Most Bills are public Bills involving measures relating to public policy. They tend to be general in character and affect everyone (though they may apply to only one of the countries of Britain). There are also private Bills, which generally apply only to one area, company or undertaking (see pp. 73-4).

Public Bills

Public Bills can be introduced in either House, by a government minister or by an ordinary ('private' or 'backbench') member, who does not hold office in the Government. Most public Bills are in practice drafted on behalf of ministers, and have the support of the Cabinet before being presented to Parliament by the appropriate minister.

Before a government Bill is drafted there may be consultation with professional bodies, voluntary organisations and other agencies interested in the subject, and interest groups and pressure groups, which seek to promote specific causes.

Proposals for legislative changes are sometimes set out in government 'White Papers', which may be debated in Parliament before a Bill is introduced. From time to time consultation papers, sometimes called 'Green Papers', set out government proposals which are still taking shape and seek comments from the public.

Bills are printed by HMSO and usually consist of:

—A short title—the name by which the Bill is generally known.

—A long title summarising the purpose of the Bill.

—A preamble describing the desirability of legislating on the subject. This is rare nowadays in a public Bill.

—The clauses of the Bill, containing the main provisions.

—The schedules, which contain detailed matters dependent on the provisions of the Bill: for instance, lists of laws to be repealed by the Bill.

A Bill may be accompanied by a memorandum in non-technical language, explaining its contents and objectives. Government Bills providing for the expenditure of public money must have a financial memorandum and must describe the effect of the Bill on public service manpower.

Public Bills can be introduced in either House. As a rule, however, government Bills likely to raise political controversy go through the Commons before being discussed in the Lords, while those of a technical but non-political nature often pass through the Lords first. (Those dealing with law consolidation and law reform are always introduced in the House of Lords.) If a Bill has a mainly financial purpose it is nearly always introduced in the Commons, and a Bill involving taxation or the spending of public money must be based on resolutions agreed by the Commons, often after debate, before it can be introduced. If the main object of a Bill is to create a public charge (that is, new taxation or public spending), it must be introduced by a government minister in the Commons. If brought from the Lords it can only proceed in the Commons if taken up by a minister. This gives the Government considerable control over legislation.

Legislation introduced in the House of Commons is often revised by amendments passed in the House of Lords. The House of Lords and the House of Commons are equally responsible for private Bills (see pp. 73-4) and for delegated legislation (although statutory instruments on financial matters are not laid before the House of Lords).

Government Bills and government amendments to Bills are drafted by parliamentary draftsmen, also known as parliamentary counsel. These are barristers and solicitors who are established civil servants. The parliamentary draftsmen for Scotland are on the staff of the Lord Advocate's Department.

The process of passing a public Bill is similar in both Houses.

Procedure in the House of Commons

The stages through which a Bill has to pass are intended to provide opportunities not only for consideration, but for reconsideration. The stages are as follows:

—first reading;[26]

—second reading;

[26]Although Bills are no longer read aloud, the stages are still known as readings. This is a reminder of the days when printed copies were not generally available, and the contents of a Bill were read out by a clerk.

—committee;

—report; and

—third reading.

The stages follow at intervals of between one day and several weeks, depending on the nature of the Bill. In the House of Commons, the report and third reading are usually taken on the same day. In exceptional circumstances, all the stages may be taken on the same day. Although treated as parts of a single process, each stage is regarded as having a particular function which, to some extent, limits the range of debate.

First Reading

The first reading of a public Bill is a formality. The Bill may be presented and read for the first time as a result of the House agreeing to a motion to introduce it, or it may simply be introduced, read for the first time and ordered to be read a second time. Once presented, it is printed and proceeds to a second reading.

Second Reading

The second reading provides the first main occasion for debate on the general principles of a Bill; alternative methods of achieving its purposes and the means proposed for giving effect to its provisions may be raised. Detailed discussion, including criticisms which could be met by amendment, is reserved for the committee, or report, stage. The Opposition may decide to vote against the Bill on its second reading, or to move an amendment to the motion that the Bill be read a second time, in order to save time in the Chamber. Similarly, public Bills relating exclusively to Scotland or Wales may, in certain circumstances, be referred by the House of

Commons to the Scottish or Welsh Grand Committee for the second reading stage (see p. 84). When this happens, the second reading committee must report that it has considered the principle of the Bill. The Bill thus returned to the House has not been read a second time, but subsequently a formal motion to give it a second reading is considered without debate. If this motion is passed, the Bill is considered to have been read a second time. The Bill is then generally committed to a standing committee for detailed discussion.

Committee Stage

When a Bill has passed its second reading, it is usually referred to a standing committee consisting of from 16 to 50 MPs for detailed examination (see p. 83). Occasionally the Bill may be referred to the whole House, sitting in committee. This is often the case, for instance, with Bills of constitutional importance and with parts of the Finance Bills which include Budget proposals. Very occasionally a Bill will go to a select committee or to a special standing committee. These have the power to call witnesses.

The object of the committee stage is to study the details of a measure; the Bill is dealt with clause by clause and its individual provisions may be altered, provided that this is in keeping with the principle of the Bill, which the House is taken to have affirmed on second reading. In committee an MP may speak as often as he or she wishes instead of only once as in other debates. Members may intervene and cross-examine quite freely in order to pursue complex points and to seek to ensure that the text of the Bill is consistent. The 16 large committee rooms in the Committee Corridor (above the libraries of the two Houses), where six or more committees may be examining Bills, are one of the busiest parts of the Palace of Westminster.

Report Stage

During the report stage the House considers the Bill as amended; it may also make further amendments. The report stage is, in practice, very like the committee stage, except that only the amendments and not the clauses of the Bill are discussed and all members may speak and vote.

A timetable for the committee and remaining stages of certain Bills may be agreed voluntarily between the parties or, failing this, the House may vote to limit the time devoted to examining a Bill by passing a government timetable motion, commonly known as a 'guillotine'. This lays down precisely how much time is to be allotted for each stage of a Bill (and, sometimes, which of its clauses are to be debated on a particular day).

Third Reading

At the third reading a Bill is reviewed in its final form, which includes the amendments made at earlier stages. Substantive amendments cannot be made at this stage. The third reading is generally short. After the third reading a Commons Bill is sent to the Lords.

Procedure in the House of Lords

House of Lords procedure is broadly similar to that in the Commons. When a Bill is brought from the Commons or introduced into the Lords, the first reading is moved at once, and the Bill goes through the same stages as in the Commons. There are no second reading committees or standing committees, and Bills normally go through committee stage in a Committee of the whole House. There may be a report stage even when no amendments have been made in committee, and amendments may be moved then and on third reading. A Bill which starts in the Lords and is passed by that House is then sent to the Commons for all its stages there. Although Bills have formally to be passed by both Houses, in practice financial legislation is not scrutinised in detail by the Lords.

Amendments in the Second House

If the second House to consider the Bill amends it, it must be returned to the House where it originated for consideration of the amendments. If the first House rejects the amendments made by the second House, a committee is set up to list the reasons for the disagreement. Alternatively, the second House may simply propose amendments to those sent by the first House. The disputed amendments may then be dropped or insisted upon, or alternative amendments proposed. The process continues—with formal messages passing between the two Houses regarding Bills and amendments—until agreement is reached. If it proves impossible to reach agreement, the Bill is lost; but the Commons can use their powers under the Parliament Acts 1911 and 1949 (see p. 26) to present a Bill originating in the House of Commons for Royal Assent after one year and in a new session, even if the Lords' objections are maintained.

The Lords' debates can have great influence on the text of Bills; in addition, the stages in the Lords give the Government further opportunities to introduce amendments arising from points which may have been raised during the Commons' debates.

The assent of the House of Lords is not essential, subject to certain conditions, in the case of 'money Bills'. These include financial Bills such as the Finance Bill which authorises taxation, and the Consolidated Fund or Appropriation Bill which authorises national expenditure. Bills dealing solely with taxation or expenditure must become law within one month of being sent to the Lords, whether or not the Lords agree to it, unless the Commons directs otherwise.

Royal Assent

When a Bill has completed its parliamentary stages, it is sent to the Sovereign for Royal Assent. Royal Assent takes the form of an announcement rather than any signature or mark on the copy of the Bill. The Sovereign signifies assent by Letters Patent;[27] this is generally declared to both Houses by their Speakers, and, at the end of each session, by a Royal Commission which covers prorogation as well as Bills awaiting Royal Assent. After this the Bill becomes part of the law of the land and is known as an Act of Parliament. The Royal Assent has not been refused since 1707 (see footnote p. 3).

Private Members' Bills

A private member's Bill is a public Bill introduced by a private member (backbencher)—that is, a member of either House who is not a member of the Government.

At the beginning of each session, private members of the Commons ballot (draw lots) for the opportunity to introduce a Bill on one of the Fridays specially allocated for unofficial Bills; the first 20 are successful. Private members may also present a Bill (usually after Question Time—see p. 87).

A member may also seek to introduce a Bill under the 'ten-minute' rule. This allows the proposer to make a brief speech in favour of his or her measure and an objector a few minutes to say why the proposed Bill should not proceed, after which the House decides whether to allow it to be brought in. Bills introduced under

[27]Letters, delivered open and with the Great Seal attached, containing public directions from the Sovereign.

the ten-minute rule are seldom serious attempts at legislation. The process is used much more as a way of making a point about the need to change the law on a particular matter.

Private members' Bills are not always debated, due to pressure on parliamentary time; and many of those which are debated proceed no further than second reading. However a few become law in each session.

Private members' Bills do not often call for the expenditure of public money, but if they do they cannot proceed to committee stage unless the Government decides to provide the necessary money resolution.

Private members' Bills may be introduced in the House of Lords at any time during the session, without a ballot but when they come to the Commons they do not proceed further unless taken up by a private member. They must then take their turn behind private members' Bills which have already obtained a second reading in the Commons.

The success of a private member's Bill may be measured in other ways, besides progress in legislation. Bills are sometimes withdrawn or allowed to lapse if the Government states that it will set up an inquiry into the subject, or if it undertakes to introduce legislation at a later date, to the satisfaction of the sponsor of the Bill. With some Bills, the sponsor may consider the publicity to be more valuable than actual legislative results.

Private and Hybrid Bills

A private Bill, which is quite different from a private member's Bill, is legislation which applies only to part of the community, as distinct from the community as a whole. The great majority of private Bills are local in character and the promoters are mainly local

Her Majesty Queen Elizabeth II and His Royal Highness The Duke of Edinburgh receiving the addresses of both Houses of Parliament on the occasion of the Tercentenary of the Revolution of 1688 (see p. 16). The ceremony took place in Westminster Hall (see p. 114).

An aerial view of the Palace of Westminster (see sketch plan of the Palace on p. 115).

The Palace of Westminster as seen from across the River Thames.

The interior of the House of Lords in session (see p. 28).

The interior of the House of Commons during a debate (see p. 32).

COI Pictures

The Speaker of the House of Commons, the Rt Hon Betty Boothroyd, MP, elected in 1992. Miss Boothroyd is the first woman to be elected to the Office.

Lord Runcie (centre), the former Archbishop of Canterbury, before his introduction to the House of Lords as a newly-created life peer. Also shown are (left to right) the Garter King of Arms, Black Rod (see p. 31) and Lord Runcie's supporters in the introduction ceremony, Lord Belstead (a Conservative peer) and Lord Cledwyn of Penrhos (a Labour peer).

The Prime Minister, the Rt Hon John Major, MP, speaking in the House of Commons. The proceedings of the House of Commons have been televised since 1989 (see p. 109).

Press Association

Members of Parliament (left to right) Simon Hughes (Liberal Democrat), Dame Janet Fookes (Conservative) and Ron Davies (Labour) outside Parliament with a petition to the European Council of Ministers concerning the treatment of animals transported for slaughter. Organisations and groups of individuals frequently seek the support of MPs to bring about changes in policy.

The Reform Bill of 1832 (see p. 22) receiving the Royal Assent in the Court of Requests in the old House of Lords; engraving after S. W. Reynolds.

authorities, statutory bodies such as water companies or railways, or private companies. Occasionally they legislate for personal issues involving estates, marriage, divorce or naturalisation, but this is now rare. The provisions of a private Bill may be in excess of, and sometimes in conflict with, the general law. The coming into force of the Transport and Works Act 1992 has changed the basis on which statutory authority for major infrastructure developments will be obtained in future. Projects such as railways, tramways, ports, harbours and barrages will in most cases no longer come before Parliament for approval by way of a private Bill, but by ministerial orders following, in most cases, public local enquiries conducted by professional departmental inspectors. Parliamentary select committees will no longer hear and determine the case for such "works Bills" and the petitions against all or part of them.

Procedure

The procedure for private Bills is different from that for public Bills. While a public Bill is either presented direct to the House or introduced on a motion by an MP, a private Bill is introduced through a petition presented to Parliament by the person or organisation who desires the Bill.

Private bills are drafted by Parliamentary Agents, who are solicitors in private practice authorised by the two Houses to carry out this kind of work. A petition for a Bill is subject to scrutiny before it is accepted, to see that standing orders governing notices, advertisements, the deposit of plans and so forth, have been complied with. On acceptance, the Bill may be started in either House and goes through the same stages as a public Bill. If the House in which it was presented objects to the principle of a private Bill it can be rejected on the second reading; otherwise it is referred to committee, where most of the work is done. Petitions may be lodged against the Bill by individuals or other bodies affected by its provisions. Proceedings in committee resemble those in a court of law: promoters must prove the need for the powers or privileges they seek, and objections on the part of opposing interests are heard. Both parties may be legally represented. If the committee is satisfied with the case for the Bill, it is reported back to the House to go through its further stages.

Unlike public Bills, private Bills may be carried over from one session to the next. Similar numbers of private Bills are introduced into the two Houses, and the role of the Lords in scrutinising them is as great as that of the Commons.

Hybrid Bills

A hybrid Bill is a type of public Bill which may in certain respects affect the specific private rights of people or bodies (for instance, a Bill to make possible construction of a major bridge or tunnel might affect some privately owned land). The passage of such Bills through Parliament is governed by a special procedure which allows those affected to lodge their objections and appear before a parliamentary committee to make representations. Hybrid Bills are generally introduced by the Government.

There is some overlap between the subjects dealt with by the public, private or hybrid Bill procedure. Bills brought in by the Government which propose to undertake works of national importance, but in a local area, are generally hybrid: for example, the Bill to authorise construction of the Channel Tunnel, which received Royal Assent in 1987. On average about five or six hybrid Bills are presented every decade.

Record Copies of Acts

After Royal Assent, printed copies of the Acts are published. In addition, two master copies of all Acts, both public and private, are printed. One is sent to the Public Record Office to join the government records; the other is preserved in the Victoria Tower at the House of Lords alongside 3 million other records of the two Houses and many collections of papers of peers and members of the Commons. All are in the care of the House of Lords Record Office, which is open to the public throughout the year (see p. 126).

About 100 Acts of Parliament are passed each year.

Commencement Orders

Some Acts are brought into force immediately, some at a date specified in the Act and others by Commencement Orders (or by any combination of these methods), which may bring into force all or part of the Act. There may be more than one such order for parts of certain Acts, and some Acts may not be brought into force for a considerable time. Commencement Orders are statutory instruments (see below).

Delegated Legislation

While the primary domestic legislation of the country is carried through Parliament in the form of Bills which become Acts of Parliament, these Acts do not always contain detailed regulations. In order to reduce unnecessary pressure on parliamentary time, primary legislation often gives ministers or other authorities the power to regulate administrative details by means of secondary or 'delegated' legislation, most of which takes the form of Orders in

Council, Regulations and Rules known as statutory instruments. These instruments are as much the law of the land as the Act of Parliament from which they are derived. Statutory instruments are normally drafted by the legal department of the ministry concerned, and they may be subject, when in draft, to consultations with interested bodies and parties. There are about 2,000 statutory instruments each year; like Acts of Parliament, some statutory instruments apply to the whole of Britain, some only to one country.

For further details on delegated legislation, see pp. 98-9.

Parliamentary Committees

Both Houses of Parliament have a system of committees. It comprises:

—committees of the whole House;

—select committees;

—House of Commons standing committees on public Bills;

—joint committees of both Houses sitting and voting together; and

—private Bill committees.

Committees of the Whole House

Either House may pass a resolution setting itself up as a committee of the whole House to consider Bills in detail, clause by clause, after their second reading. This procedure is used for nearly all public Bills in the House of Lords,[28] but in the Commons it is used only if a motion is carried to resolve the House into such a committee.[29] Proceedings in committee of the whole House are conducted on the

[28]In the House of Lords the committee stage may be dispensed with by a motion to negative it after second reading or, if no amendments are tabled and no single Lord objects, by discharging the order of commitment on the day when the committee stage would have taken place.

[29]House of Commons Standing Orders provide that a public Bill (other than a Consolidated Fund or an Appropriation Bill) shall be committed to a standing committee, unless the House orders otherwise. A motion to commit a Bill to a committee of the whole House or to a select or special standing committee, or to a joint committee of the Lords and Commons, may be proposed by any member of the House.

lines normally followed by the House, except that the committee is presided over by a chairman instead of the Speaker (the Chairman of Ways and Means in the Commons, and the Chairman of Committees in the Lords). Members may speak more than once on each question.

Select Committees

Select committees are generally set up to help Parliament with the control of the executive by examining aspects of public policy and administration. They may also undertake more specific responsibilities related to the internal procedures of Parliament. They examine subjects by taking written and oral evidence and, after private deliberation, present a report to the House. There are 15 committees established by the House of Commons to examine the expenditure, administration and policy of most of the main government departments and related bodies. These cover:

—Agriculture;

—Defence;

—Education;

—Employment;

—Environment;

—Foreign Affairs;

—Health;

—Home Affairs;

—National Heritage;

—Science and Technology;

—Social Security;

—Trade and Industry;

—Transport; and

—Treasury and Civil Service.

There are also select committees on Scottish Affairs and on Welsh Affairs. In March 1994 the Commons voted in favour of setting up a Committee on Northern Ireland Affairs to oversee a range of responsibilities of the Secretary of State for Northern Ireland. A Liaison Committee considers general matters relating to the work of select committees.

The select committees on Foreign Affairs, Home Affairs, and the Treasury and Civil Service may also each appoint separate sub-committees to deal with particular subjects—for example, overseas development, race relations and immigration and the Civil Service.

Other regular Commons committees include:

—the Public Accounts Committee, which examines all government appropriation accounts, together with the relevant reports of the Comptroller and Auditor General (the chairman of the committee is traditionally a member of the official Opposition party);

—the Committee of Privileges, which meets only when a matter of parliamentary privilege is referred to it (see p. 104);

—the Select Committee on the Parliamentary Commissioner for Administration (see pp. 107-8); and

—the Select Committee on European Legislation, etc. (see p. 100).

—Four domestic select committees cover the internal workings of Parliament.

The Committee of Selection chooses members to serve on standing and select committees. Other committees, including the Standing Orders Committee, have duties relating to private Bills.

Select committees are constituted on a party basis in approximate proportion to party strength in the House. In the Lords no rule exists for limiting the number of members, but in the Commons membership of select committees is generally restricted to 15 and that of departmental select committees to a maximum of 11 (13 on the Scottish Affairs Committee), unless the House decides otherwise on a motion.

The Committee of Selection is responsible for putting a motion to the House nominating those who are to serve on select committees. In preparing its list it consults, among others, the Whips of the various parties. The names of all the members chosen are put to the House and usually agreed to without debate. In the Commons the committees choose their own chairmen or women from both the government and opposition parties, but in the Lords the chairman or woman is usually nominated by the House.

Select committees appointed by the House of Commons are usually empowered to summon witnesses to give evidence or to produce documents. The House of Lords does not give its select committees these powers automatically. In general, witnesses attend and documents are produced at the request of the committee, but, if necessary, an Order of the House may be made. Members of the public are usually allowed to be present while evidence is being given before a select committee on matters of public importance, but are always excluded during the deliberative stage. Members of the House of Commons may attend all sittings of Commons select committees but usually withdraw if requested. Lords may not attend a meeting of a Lords select committee during deliberation unless invited by the committee. In general, select committees bring before Parliament and the public, through their hearings and published reports, a body of fact and informed opinion on many important issues; they build up considerable expertise in their subjects of inquiry.

In the House of Lords there are two major select committees, with several sub-committees, on the European Communities and on Science and Technology. There are also select committees on aspects of private legislation, and of the internal working of the House, together with the Appeal and Appellate Committees in which the bulk of the House's judicial work takes place. The Committee of Selection is responsible, among other things, for choosing members to serve on all committees (with the exception of some highly specialised committees).

Standing Committees

House of Commons standing committees debate and consider amendments to public Bills at the committee stage and, in certain cases, discuss them at second reading stage. They also include two Scottish standing committees; and the Scottish, Welsh, and Northern Ireland Grand Committees (see p. 81).

Ordinary standing committees do not have distinctive names and are referred to simply as Standing Committee A, B, C and so on. Unlike select committees, which are usually appointed for the lifetime of a Parliament with little change in membership, standing committees are established with new members for each Bill or subject committed to them. Each committee has a chairman and between 16 and 50 members, with the party balance reflecting as far as possible that in the House as a whole. In a normal session there are up to ten standing committees on Bills. A Second Reading Committee consists of between 20 and 80 members nominated by the Committee of Selection to consider the particular Bill referred to it (see p. 69).

The Scottish Grand Committee (which may be convened anywhere in Scotland) consists of all MPs for the 72 Scottish constituencies, with a quorum of ten. Its function is to consider:

—the principles of exclusively Scottish Bills referred to it at second reading stage;

—the Scottish estimates (see p. 94) on at least six days in any session; and

—on not more than six days, other matters relating exclusively to Scotland.

Two Scottish standing committees each consist of from 16 to 50 members as with any other standing committee, except that at least 16 members must represent Scottish constituencies. Both consider Bills relating exclusively to Scotland, at committee stage.

The Welsh Grand Committee, whose function is to consider matters relating exclusively to Wales and Bills referred to it at second reading stage, has all 38 Welsh Members, and up to five other nominated members. The Northern Ireland Grand Committee debates matters relating specifically to Northern Ireland. Northern Ireland MPs serve on the Committee as of right; other members are appointed separately for each debate.

There are two European Standing Committees, which consider European Union proposals.

The chairmen of standing committees are appointed by the Speaker from the Chairmen's Panel, which consists of members appointed by the Speaker to act as temporary chairmen of committees of the whole House. The quorum of a committee is 17 or one-third the number of its members, excluding the chairman, whichever is the less. Meetings are held on the upper floors of the House of Commons (hence occasional reference in debates on the report or third reading stages of a Bill to work done 'upstairs').

Meetings of a standing committee are almost always held in public although committees may exclude members of the public.

The Lords' equivalent to a standing committee—a Public Bill Committee—is rarely used; instead the committee stage of a Bill is taken by the House as a whole.

Special Standing Committees

Special standing committees are rarely used. They combine characteristics of select and standing committees, in that a limited number of evidence-taking sessions can be held before the normal standing committee procedure is adopted. The type of Bill traditionally referred to this type of committee has been non-controversial in party terms, but may involve new or complex questions of policy. It has been usual for the chairman of the select committee shadowing the Bill's sponsor department to chair the special standing committee during evidence-taking sessions. Members of special standing committees are nominated by the Committee of Selection; they normally include some members of the relevant select committee.

Joint Committees

Joint committees, with a membership drawn from both Houses, are appointed in each session to consider a particular subject, a particular Bill, or all Bills of a particular type—for instance, those dealing with statute law revision, consolidation and delegated legislation. A motion to appoint a joint committee to consider a particular subject may be moved in either House, and the agreement of the other House is then sought. The proposal to commit a particular Bill to a joint committee must come from the House in which the Bill originated.

The members of a joint committee are usually chosen in equal numbers by the respective Houses. The powers of the committee and the time and place of its meetings are decided by agreement between the two Houses. The chairman is elected by the committee and may be chosen from among the members nominated by either House. Decisions are taken by vote, the chairman or woman voting like any other member.

The report of a joint committee is formally presented to both Houses—by the chairman to the House to which he or she belongs, and by a member chosen by the committee to the other House. If the joint committee has been considering a Bill, the report is made to the House in which it originated.

Private Bill Committees

The membership, role and procedure of committees on private Bills depend on whether the Bill is opposed[30] or unopposed.

—The committee on an opposed Bill before the House of Commons consists of four MPs (appointed by the Committee of Selection) who must have no personal or constituency interest in the Bill.

—For an unopposed Bill, the committee consists of the Chairman of Ways and Means and a deputy chairman, and three other members chosen by the chairman from a panel appointed by the Committee of Selection at the beginning of each session.

In the House of Lords, committees on opposed Bills consist of five members; unopposed Bills are normally referred to the Chairman of Committees.

---

[30]An opposed Bill, in this sense, is not a Bill which has been opposed in Parliament, but one against which a petition has been deposited, or one which the Chairman of Ways and Means or the Chairman of Committees considers should be treated as an opposed Bill, although no petition has been presented against it.

Parliamentary Control of Government

In addition to the system of scrutiny by select committees referred to in the last chapter, the House of Commons offers a number of opportunities for the examination of government policy, both by the Opposition and by the Government's own backbenchers. As a representative of the ordinary citizen, an MP may challenge the policy put forward by a minister:[31]

—during a debate on a particular Bill, when he or she may object to its broad principles on the second reading or, as regularly happens, may put forward amendments at committee stage;

—asking parliamentary questions which ministers must answer;

—during adjournment debates; and

—during debates on 'Opposition days'.

Question Time

Question Time in the House of Commons, in its modern form, is largely a 20th century development. Until well into the 19th century Members of Parliament had almost unlimited opportunities to speak to the House in the ordinary course of events. Nowadays, when parliamentary time is taken up mainly with public business, questions are often regarded as the best means of seeking information (to which members might not otherwise have access) about the

---

[31]Challenges to departmental ministers necessarily involve the whole Government, under the principle of Cabinet collective responsibility.

Government's intentions. They are also often seen as the most effective way of raising, and perhaps resolving, grievances brought to MPs' notice by constituents. From time to time questions may be used as part of an organised campaign to bring about a change in government policy. There may also be 'inspired' questions, when a member is asked to put down a question so that the minister responsible can make a public statement.

The rules governing admissible questions are derived mainly from decisions about individual questions taken over a long period by successive Speakers, although changes in the practice and procedure of Question Time were made following a House of Commons select committee report in 1972.

Question Time usually begins at 14.30 hours (and in any case not later than 14.45) on Monday, Tuesday, Wednesday and Thursday and goes on until 15.30 hours.

The Prime Minister answers questions at 15.15 hours on Tuesdays and Thursdays every week, and other ministers answer questions in rotation on a particular day or days of the week.

Procedure

Questions are usually handed in at the Table Office[32] in writing, but may be sent by post. Usually at least two days' notice must be given to allow time for an answer to be prepared. If an oral answer is required, the question must be marked with an asterisk; questions without asterisks are answered in writing. An MP may ask up to two oral questions and any number of written questions a day. No more than eight questions requiring oral answers may be tabled by any MP during a period of ten sitting days. An MP may ask only one oral question of any one minister on any day.

[32]The Table Office consists of four Clerks who handle questions and motions under the direction of the Principal Clerk (Table Office).

The answers to written questions are printed in *Hansard,* though not necessarily on the day on which they appear on the order paper (that is, the agenda for the day's business in the House). They are also sent direct to the MPs who asked them. There is also a procedure for 'priority' written answers, whereby an MP can state that he or she wishes the answer to a written question to be printed on the day that it appears on the order paper. Oral questions that have not been reached because of lack of time receive a written answer, but broadly only those oral questions which are likely to be reached are now treated as valid notices of question; the rest are null and void.

Admissibility of Questions

Before a question is put on the order paper, it must be passed by the Table Office to see that it conforms to the rules, and it may be edited to bring it into line with parliamentary practice. Questions may relate to purely local matters or they may involve issues of national policy. In either case their admissibility is governed by principles arising from decisions made by successive Speakers of the House. Broadly speaking,

—a question must be framed as a genuine question and not as a statement or speech in the interrogative;

—it must not seek the interpretation of a statute or legal opinion;

—it must not ask for information already published or for the confirmation of a rumour or press report;

—it must not be 'tendentious, controversial, ironic, vague, frivolous or repetitive'; and

—it must be concerned with a matter for which a minister is officially responsible.

Ministers are not responsible for the activities of local authorities or nationalised (or privatised) industries, although they do answer questions on national statistics. Members are not prohibited from agreeing to table questions on the same topic on a particular day and there is nothing to prevent other MPs responding to such questions with questions of their own.

Ministers' Answers

Answers to questions are prepared in the department of the minister concerned, but the minister is personally responsible for both oral and written replies. The minister always answers questions put to him or her unless there are strong reasons (for example, on grounds of national security) for not doing so. If a minister refuses to take the action or give the information asked for in a question, the same question may be put again in three months' time. There are a number of subjects such as the security services or matters of commercial confidence on which ministers in successive administrations have consistently refused to answer questions. Where a refusal prevents a question from being admitted on such a subject, ministers may be asked once every session whether they would now be prepared to answer such questions. As a result governments have to review their policies regularly in regard to their refusal to answer certain questions; their refusal to answer at a particular time does not mean that the issue is closed.

Supplementary Questions

An MP who feels that the answer to his or her oral question needs clarifying is entitled, at the discretion of the Speaker, to ask a further or 'supplementary' question or questions. These are followed by a further answer by the minister, and there may be still further questions with other MPs joining in. A notable feature of Question Time is the way in which the Speaker controls the pace; if he or she calls too many supplementary questions the minister may be subjected to close scrutiny on a few matters but the total number of questions answered orally is small; if he or she calls too few supplementary questions, on the other hand, more questions can be answered orally but the minister may have an easier passage. In an average session around 25,000 questions are tabled and answered (the rules relating to oral questions have recently been changed and a significant reduction in the number asked is anticipated). Only about 6,000 (including supplementary questions) are answered orally in the House of Commons. An oral question has been officially estimated to cost £225 and a written question £97.

Private Notice Questions

Urgent questions about matters of public importance or the arrangement of parliamentary business that have not appeared on the order paper may be taken at the end of Question Time with the Speaker's permission. Such questions are known as private notice questions; the minister concerned is always informed that they are to be put. Examples have included developments in the Gulf crisis, cold weather payments to those in need, and violence on an unusual scale or of a new type.

House of Lords

The House of Lords also has a Question Time, immediately after Prayers and formal business, but it is much briefer (30 minutes at most) than in the House of Commons, and the procedure is different. Up to four 'starred' questions may be asked at the beginning of the business each day but not more than one by any Lord. Starred questions are so called because they appear on the order paper with an asterisk against them. They are asked in order to obtain specific information, and not with a view to making a speech or raising a debate, although supplementaries may be asked. In addition, 'unstarred' (debatable) questions may be asked at the end of business on any day, when speeches may be made. The Government customarily replies at the end of the debate. Private notice questions may be asked, and any Lord may put down questions to the Government for written answer, up to a maximum of six for each peer on any day.

Adjournment Debates

An MP can use the motion for the adjournment of the House of Commons to open a discussion on an issue relating to his or her constituency or a matter of public concern. There is a half-hour adjournment period at the end of the business of the day; and immediately before the adjournment for each recess (Christmas, Easter, spring and summer breaks) a full day is spent discussing matters raised by private members.

An MP wishing to raise a matter during the half-hour adjournment period must notify the Speaker in writing. A ballot is held once a week and four MPs gain the right to speak during the following week; the Speaker chooses the subject for discussion on one day a week. The names of MPs who have been unsuccessful in the ballot and have not been chosen by the Speaker are included in subsequent ballots if they formally renew their request; successful MPs may not submit a subject again until a week has elapsed. Normally only the MP raising the matter and the minister responsible for replying speak during an adjournment debate.

Special Adjournment Motions

An MP wishing to discuss 'a specific and important matter that should have urgent consideration' may, at the end of Question Time, ask leave to move the adjournment of the House. The terms of such a motion must be given to the Speaker in writing and, if the Speaker accepts that the subject proposed for discussion is grave and urgent enough, the MP asks the House for leave for the motion to be put forward. Speakers have not, in general, allowed more than a few such requests each session. Leave can be given unanimously if 40 or more MPs support the motion, or if fewer than 40 but more than ten support it and the House (on a vote) is in favour. Once leave has been given, the matter is debated for three hours, usually on the following day. Debates on such special adjournment motions are commonly known as emergency debates.

Opposition Days

On 20 days in each parliamentary session the Opposition in the House of Commons can choose subjects for debate, giving it opportunities to criticise the Government. These Opposition days replace the 29 so-called 'supply days' which used to be regarded as Opposition time. 'Supply' is an old term which originally referred to those days during the last century when the Commons discussed details of proposed government expenditure (the 'estimates').[33]

[33]The estimates are the expected financial requirements of the public service for the coming financial year. They consist of the Defence Estimates, a number of classes of Civil Estimates and separate estimates for House of Commons administration. Each class is subdivided into votes which specify the purposes for which money is required. They are prepared by the relevant government departments and scrutinised by the Treasury which, before presenting them to the House of Commons, must weigh the advantages of administrative proposals against the monetary and economic cost. It must also decide on the relevant merits of expenditure proposed by different departments, and must eliminate overlapping, uneconomic or wasteful expenditure.

Under changes which came into force in 1982, certain topics traditionally dealt with in Opposition time, which occupied a total of nine days, are now taken in government time, and thus the balance between government and Opposition time remains largely unchanged. Of these days, 17 are at the disposal of the Leader of the Opposition and three at the disposal of the second-largest opposition party.

Estimates Days

Three days are set aside each year for debates on details of proposed government expenditure chosen by the Liaison Committee. (The Liaison Committee is made up largely of Select Committee Chairmen. It considers general matters relating to the work of Select Committees—see p. 80.)

Consolidated Fund Debates

Three times a year, after Consolidated Fund or Appropriation Bills have been passed without debate and the necessary supplies (money) for the Crown have been voted (see below), members can exercise their traditional right of 'raising grievances' on matters for which any minister is responsible. The debates last about 90 minutes each and take place throughout the night.

Financial Procedure

The main responsibilities of Parliament, and more particularly of the House of Commons, in overseeing the revenue of the State and payments for the public service, are to authorise the raising of taxes and duties, and the various objects of expenditure and the sums to be spent. It also has to satisfy itself that the sums granted are spent only for the purposes which Parliament intended. No payment out of the central Government's public funds can be made and no taxation or loans authorised, except by Act of Parliament. However limited interim payments can be made from the Contingencies Fund.

Expenditure

Some government expenditure is sanctioned by specific Acts which remain in force until they are repealed: this includes lending from the National Loans Fund to the nationalised industries, or the salaries and pensions of judges and other high officers of State. Expenditure on the supply services (which includes spending on defence, on the social services and on the general administration of the country) must, however, be sanctioned annually by the House of Commons. It is embodied in the Appropriation Act, which authorises the issue of the grants appropriating the amounts required.

In order to provide money for government expenditure between the beginning of the financial year (1 April) and the passing of the Appropriation Act in July or August, votes on account for the civil and defence departments are passed by the House in December or January. Subsequently a Consolidated Fund Act is passed authorising the sums required to be issued out of the Consolidated Fund (the fund into which all revenues are paid and from which all public expenditure issues). Supplementary estimates may also be presented if a department later considers it necessary to exceed its original estimate. Resolutions authorising the sums are voted, and the amounts embodied in the next Consolidated Fund Bill. All voted money for each financial year is appropriated to specific objects in the annual Appropriation Act. In times of emergency, for instance wartime, a 'vote of credit' not allocated to any particular object may be voted.

Revenue

Revenue, like expenditure, is raised partly under statutes that continue until repealed, and partly under the authority of annual statutes, the most important of these being the Finance Act. The legislation is based on the Chancellor of the Exchequer's Budget statement. The first new unified Budget, containing both public expenditure and taxation plans, was announced in November 1993; previously there had been a two-stage budgetary procedure: the Autumn Statement, setting out public expenditure plans and the Spring Budget containing taxation plans. Parliament thus has the opportunity to consider spending proposals alongside the proposed tax changes. Taxation changes are set out in a Finance Bill in January for detailed consideration by Parliament, with the intention of achieving Royal Assent by May.

The House of Lords debates the Finance Bill in general terms after it has been passed by the House of Commons. The Lords, however, do not examine the Bill in detail, nor do they suggest any amendments.

There may be more than one Budget and Finance Act in a year.

Scrutiny of Expenditure

The House of Commons is assisted in carrying out its responsibilities for the national finances by the Comptroller and Auditor General, and by the Public Accounts Committee and the various departmental select committees.

Comptroller and Auditor General

The Comptroller and Auditor General, an officer of the House of Commons, appointed by the Crown, has two distinct functions:

—As Comptroller General he or she is responsible for ensuring that all revenue and other public money payable to the Consolidated Fund and the National Loans Fund is duly paid and that all payments from these funds are authorised by statute.

—As Auditor General he or she must certify the accounts of all government departments and executive agencies, as well as those of a wide range of other public sector bodies; scrutinise the economy, efficiency and effectiveness of their operations; examine revenue accounts and inventories; and report the results of these examinations to Parliament.

Public Accounts Committee

The Public Accounts Committee was originally set up in 1861 to ensure that all public money was spent as Parliament had intended. These terms of reference have been widely interpreted by successive Committees, which have investigated whether full value has been obtained for the sums spent by departments, and have reported in detail on cases in which administration has appeared faulty or negligent. The Committee has therefore become a powerful instrument for exposing waste and inefficiency. It sets out its findings in regular reports to Parliament. Although the Committee has no executive powers, its reports carry considerable weight and its recommendations are taken seriously by the departments and organisations that it examines. The Government's formal reply to these reports is presented to Parliament by the Treasury in the form of Treasury minutes. The reports and minutes are debated annually in the House of Commons. The Committee is traditionally chaired by a senior member of the main opposition party.

Control of Delegated Legislation

Procedures exist to enable Parliament to scrutinise the use of delegated legislation. This is the system which, in order to reduce unnecessary pressure on parliamentary time, gives ministers and other authorities the power to regulate administrative details, mainly in the form of statutory instruments (SIs) after a law has been passed. (See p. 77.)

To minimise any risk that delegating powers to the executive might undermine the authority of Parliament, such powers are normally delegated only to authorities directly accountable to Parliament. Moreover the Acts of Parliament by which particular powers are delegated usually provide for some measure of direct parliamentary control over the delegated legislation, by giving Parliament the opportunity to affirm or annul it. Certain Acts require that specific organisations must be consulted before rules and orders can be made.

The majority of SIs are not subject to any parliamentary procedure and therefore become law on the date stated in them; some are not even laid before Parliament for information. Other SIs are subject to parliamentary proceedings; these are of two main types:

—*an affirmative instrument* must be specifically approved by both Houses (or by the Commons alone if it is a financial matter) before it can come into force. Many important SIs fall into this category; and

—*a negative instrument* is laid before Parliament and comes into force automatically unless either House (or the Commons only in the case of instruments dealing with financial matters) within 40 days passes a motion, called a prayer, annulling it. There are more negative instruments than affirmative ones.

Parliament can only reject or accept statutory instruments; it cannot amend or adapt them, except in very rare cases where the parent Act provides otherwise. Parliament simply expresses its wish for them to either be annulled or passed into law. The procedure to be applied, to any particular statutory instrument is laid down in the parent Act. Since the Parliament Acts 1911 and 1949 do not apply to delegated legislation, the Commons cannot override the Lords in this area.

A Joint Select Committee on Statutory Instruments, made up of members of both Houses, considers all SIs laid before Parliament. The Commons members of the joint committee consider by themselves instruments laid before that House only. Like other select committees, the Committee may take oral or written evidence from the appropriate government department. The Committee's scrutiny is purely technical: it may not consider the merits of any SI, but merely ensures that it conforms to the provisions of the parent Act and is properly drafted. The Committee comments on a significant number of SIs but does so only to provide Parliament with information. Even when it does report that an SI goes beyond the power of its parent Act, neither Parliament nor the Government is obliged to taken any action.

In order to save time on the floor of the House (that is, the main debating chamber, as opposed to the committee rooms), the Commons also uses standing committees to debate the merits of instruments; actual decisions are taken by the House as a whole.

A recent innovation in the House of Lords is the establishment, on an experimental basis, of a new Select Committee on the Scrutiny of Delegated Powers. This advises the Lords on the appropriate level of delegated powers in the legislation before it.

Parliament and Executive Agencies

Executive agencies are separate units within the Civil Service responsible for performing executive functions of government.

They are being created under the Next Steps Initiative, which was launched in 1988 with the aim of improving management in the Civil Service and the quality of services provided to the public and to customers within government. Under the terms of a framework document agencies enjoy greater delegation on financial, pay and personnel matters. Examples include the Employment Service and the United Kingdom Passport Agency. By December 1993 92 executive agencies had been created, employing 60 per cent of the Civil Service.

While ministers remain accountable to Parliament for the policies of executive agencies, the agency chief executives normally reply to letters from MPs or written parliamentary questions on operational matters within their responsibility. These replies are published in *Hansard*.

Parliament and the European Union

Arrangements have been made in both Houses of Parliament to keep members informed of European Union developments and to enable them to scrutinise and debate proposals for Community legislation and other policies before they are fully approved by the Council of the European Union.

Select Committees

Both Houses of Parliament have select committees which examine proposals for Community legislation and other Community documents. In the Commons there is the Select Committee on European Legislation. The equivalent body in the House of Lords is the Select Committee on the European Communities. Both committees automatically receive all draft proposals for legislation which has been submitted to the Council of the European Union. The government department concerned also provides an explanatory memorandum describing the subject matter and its implications for Britain.

House of Commons Select Committee on European Legislation
The Commons committee helps Members of Parliament identify important proposals which affect matters of principle or policy, or involve changes in British law. Government ministers and civil servants may be invited to give evidence to the committee and a senior official of the House assists it in dealing with the legal implications of proposals. Further legal advice may be given, where necessary, by the Government's Law Officers. If the committee recommends that a proposal be debated by the House before a final decision is taken by the Council, the Government finds time for the debate. The House may also send documents to two European Standing Committees where they can be debated.

House of Lords Select Committee on the European Communities
The terms of reference of the Lords committee are more widely drawn, for it can report on the merits of Community proposals of legal or political importance. The proposals are remitted as necessary to one of several specialist sub-committees, which may call for oral or written evidence from the Government and appropriate outside bodies. The legal implications of Community proposals are examined by a sub-committee chaired by a law lord. Reports are made to the House and, as in the Commons, time is found for debate.

Other Means of Information
Members of the Commons can obtain copies of European Community documents and information through services provided

by the House of Commons Department of the Library and the European section of the Overseas Office in the Department of the Clerk of the House. In addition, explanatory memoranda are provided by the Government on each legislative proposal made to the Council by the Commission of the European Community. Copies of these memoranda are made available to members of the House through the Library and Vote Office.

Every month when Parliament is sitting a report is made by the minister responsible in the Foreign & Commonwealth Office, listing all the Council meetings due to be held in the coming month and the subjects expected to be discussed at each meeting. After each Council meeting the minister who attended reports to the Commons, usually in the form of a parliamentary written answer, on the discussions that took place. After each meeting of the European Council of heads of Government the Prime Minister reports to the House of Commons, and is questioned.

Every six months the Government publishes a White Paper summarising developments in the European Union and giving an indication of the Government's general approach and policy on specific issues. A debate on the White Paper is then held in the House of Commons; this provides an opportunity for wide-ranging discussion on Union developments.

Members of both Houses of Parliament may table questions on any Union topic for written or oral answer by the appropriate minister.

Similar arrangements for papers and for statements and questions on the floor of the House have been made in the Lords.

The Commons' Ability to Force the Government to Resign

Control of the Government is finally exercised by the ability of the House of Commons to force the Government to resign, by passing a resolution of 'no confidence' or by rejecting a proposal which the Government considers so vital to its policy that it has made it a matter of confidence. It could also refuse to vote the money needed for the public service.

Parliamentary Privilege

Each House of Parliament has rights and immunities to protect it from obstruction in carrying out its duties. These rights apply collectively to each House and to its staff and individually to each member.

For the Commons, the Speaker formally claims from the Queen their 'ancient and undoubted rights and privileges' at the beginning of each Parliament. These include freedom of speech; first call on the attendance of its members, who are therefore free from arrest in civil actions and exempt from serving on juries, or being compelled to attend courts as witnesses or serving as sheriffs; and the right of access to the Crown, which is a collective privilege of the House. Parliamentary privilege forms a special kind of law—interpreted and administered within the walls of Parliament, but acknowledged and recognised everywhere as part of the law of the land.

Further privileges include the rights of the House to control its own proceedings (so that it may, for instance, exclude 'strangers' if it wishes);[34] to decide upon legal disqualifications for membership and to declare a seat vacant on such grounds; and to punish for breach of its privileges and for contempt.

Freedom of Speech

The most important privilege is that of freedom of speech. When MPs are speaking to fellow members, they enjoy a complete right of free speech, subject only to the rules of order administered by the

[34] All those who are not members or officials of either House.

Speaker. MPs cannot be prosecuted for sedition or sued for libel or slander over anything said during proceedings in the House or published on its order paper. This means that it is possible to raise in the House questions affecting the public good which might be difficult to raise outside owing to the possibility of being sued under the law of defamation. Such privilege is not a personal favour to individual MPs, but instead is seen as necessary protection and a guarantee that they should be able to defend to the full the interests of the electors. Thus the privilege of MPs is regarded as the privilege of every citizen.

Breach of Privilege

Parliament has the right to punish anybody, inside or outside the House, who commits a breach of privilege—that is, offends against the rights of the House. Nowadays, an MP complaining of an alleged breach of privilege must submit the case privately to the Speaker, who then decides whether the matter can be raised in the Chamber itself. If this is done at the earliest opportunity and if the Speaker agrees and rules in the House that a case appears to have been established, the matter takes precedence over all other business. No other business can be transacted until the House has either dealt with the alleged breach itself, or referred it to the Committee of Privileges (see p. 81), which investigates the matter and reports to the House. If, when summoned, an offender admits the offence but offers a full apology, the Committee often recommends that it be accepted. The House then considers the Committee's report and decides whether or not the offender should be punished.

Punishment for Contempt

Parliament claims the right to punish not only breaches of its privileges, but also 'contempt', which is any offence or libel against its dignity or authority. An offender may be imprisoned in the precincts of the House, though this penalty has not been imposed since 1880. Nowadays the House would probably order offenders to be reprimanded. Offenders who are not MPs are brought to the Bar by the Serjeant at Arms, where they are reprimanded by the Speaker in the name, and by the authority, of the House. If the offender is an MP, he or she receives the Speaker's reprimand standing in his or her place. An offending MP may also be suspended or, in extreme cases, expelled from the House. Other offenders may be ordered to attend at the Bar of the House; all may put their case about their offences or seek to reduce their punishment before the House decides what action to take.

Privileges of the House of Lords

The privileges of the House of Lords include: freedom of speech in debate; freedom of access to the Sovereign for each peer individually; and the right to punish individuals for contempt. These privileges are not formally claimed by the Speaker as in the House of Commons, but they exist independently.

Parliament and the Citizen

Individual citizens, who help choose the Government by voting at elections, have direct contact with Parliament through the MPs for their constituencies. It is an MP's duty to represent all his or her constituents and, where necessary, to pursue their grievances by contacting the government departments concerned, by raising the matter in the House of Commons through parliamentary questions or by asking for an adjournment debate, or by referring it to the Parliamentary Commissioner (see below). MPs also help their constituents on matters where legislation affects them. All MPs receive correspondence from constituents with problems, often involving conflict with government departments. Most also hold regular advice bureaux or 'surgeries', where constituents can consult them in person.

The Parliamentary Commissioner for Administration

The Parliamentary Commissioner for Administration (the 'Ombudsman') is an officer of the House of Commons, independent of the Government. The Commissioner's function is to investigate complaints of alleged maladministration when asked to do so by MPs on behalf of members of the public. Powers of investigation extend to administrative actions by staff in central government departments and certain executive and non-departmental bodies. They do not include policy decisions (which can be questioned in Parliament) and matters affecting relations with other countries. Complaints by British citizens arising from dealings with British posts overseas can be investigated in some circumstances. The Commissioner does not normally investigate cases where alternative remedies through proceedings in the courts of law or appeal to an administrative tribunal exist. He or she has discretion, however, to take on exceptional cases when satisfied that it is not reasonable to use an alternative remedy.

The Commissioner has access to all departmental papers and reports the findings of his or her investigation to the MP who presented the complaint. The Commissioner reports annually to Parliament and in addition publishes details of selected investigations at quarterly intervals and may submit other reports where necessary.

A House of Commons select committee oversees the Commissioner's work, takes evidence if it wishes from heads of departments and others, and reports to the House.

Information About the Work of Parliament

Hansard

In both Houses of Parliament an official report of the day's proceedings is published the following morning (and also in weekly versions and in bound volumes published periodically during a session). The reports are commonly known as *Hansard* after the name of the family of printers and publishers who published parliamentary papers in the 19th century. As well as a transcript of proceedings on the floor of both Houses, each daily report includes the answers to parliamentary questions put down for a written reply. (A Hansard of the debates in each standing committee is also published.)

Further Information

Every Saturday when in session, the House of Commons publishes a *Weekly Information Bulletin* giving details of the business for the past and the coming week (including future business in the Lords), the state of legislation and information about other parliamentary affairs.

The Information Office in the House of Lords provides information for the public as well as for members. Enquiries about aspects of the work of the House of Lords may be directed to the Clerk (see below).

The House of Commons has a Public Information Office to answer enquiries on all aspects of the work and history of the House of Commons, and to make available a series of publications.[35] In particular, a series of over 60 factsheets (available free) describes various aspects of the House's work and procedure. An Education Officer for both Houses is attached to this Office, and makes available a series of leaflets and wallcharts, and, with the help of the Central Office of Information, supplies audio-visual aids for use in schools.

The records of the Lords from 1497 and of the Commons from 1547, together with the parliamentary and political papers of certain past members of both Houses, are available to the public in the House of Lords Record Office. A general guide to the records of Parliament has been published (see Further Reading, p. 145).

Broadcasting of Parliament

The proceedings of both Houses may be broadcast on television and radio. Radio broadcasting of some of the proceedings of both Houses of Parliament began in 1978. Televising of the proceedings of the House of Lords began in 1985; proceedings of the House of Commons have been televised since 1989, subject to controls,

[35]Enquiries should be addressed to: Public Information Office, House of Commons, London SW1A 0AA (telephone: 071-219 4272) or the Information Office, House of Lords, London SW1A 0PW (telephone: 071-219 3107). Educational enquiries are dealt with on 071–219 4750.

imposed by the House, on the nature of the coverage. Recorded extracts of proceedings are used extensively on news and current affairs programmes on television and radio. Certain special proceedings are broadcast live for example, the presentation of the Budget by the Chancellor of the Exchequer, or Prime Minister's Question Time.

Radio and television recordings of past debates in both Houses and also some standing committees and select committee hearings are kept in archives. At present the recordings are available only to members and officials of both Houses under the control of the two select committees on Broadcasting. These committees also review issues relating to broadcasting.

When Parliament is in session BBC Radio 4 is obliged to broadcast an impartial day-by-day account of the proceedings of both Houses of Parliament. This is the evening programme *Today in Parliament* and its re-edited version *Yesterday in Parliament*, broadcast the following morning. Other weekly programmes on BBC Radio 4 include *In Committee*, which examines the proceedings of the House of Commons departmental select committees; and the series, *The Week in Westminster*, which invites MPs to comment on aspects of the week's parliamentary affairs. Weekly programmes on parliamentary affairs are broadcast on a number of independent local radio stations. Capital Radio, for example, engages alternately a Conservative or a Labour MP from a London constituency to sum up the week's affairs in *Party Pieces*.

BBC television broadcasts *Westminster Live*, which covers the previous day's proceedings in Parliament, while *Scrutiny* covers the work of committees; and regional weekly programmes concentrate on the work of local MPs. Channel 4's programmes include *House to House* and *A Week in Politics*.

On satellite television BSkyB's *Parliament Live* covers the House of Commons proceedings daily and also broadcasts a weekly programme *The Lords This Week*. Full coverage in the form of the Parliamentary Channel is available on cable television.

Newspaper Coverage of Parliament

Most national and regional newspapers in Britain have parliamentary correspondents who report debates in Parliament from the press galleries of the House of Commons and the House of Lords. In the Commons the gallery above the Speaker's chair seats reporters employed by Hansard, the newspapers, press agencies, radio and television organisations, accredited correspondents from other Commonwealth and foreign countries, and members of 'the Lobby'. These are political correspondents with access to the Members' Lobby of the House of Commons, where they can talk privately to government ministers and other members of the House. (The leading national and provincial newspapers and the broadcasting media each have lobby correspondents.) Coverage of parliamentary affairs is given by the press as a whole, and five national newspapers present a daily summary of the previous day's proceedings in both Houses.

Each year many new books, pamphlets and feature articles deal with aspects of parliamentary life.

The Hansard Society

The Hansard Society for Parliamentary Government—an unofficial, non-party, educational society—promotes interest in the institutions of parliamentary government. Membership is open to corporate bodies and individuals. The Society's activities include holding meetings, maintaining an information service, and publishing books, pamphlets and a quarterly survey, *Parliamentary Affairs*.

The Buildings of the Houses of Parliament

The Houses of Parliament occupy the site of a former royal palace, the Palace of Westminster, which was the principal residence of the kings of England from the middle of the 11th century to 1512. Little remains of the original buildings except Westminster Hall, begun by William II in 1097 and enlarged by Richard II at the end of the 14th century. The official title of the building remains the Palace of Westminster and certain ceremonial rooms continue to be controlled directly by the Queen's representative, the Lord Great Chamberlain.

In medieval times kings summoned their courts wherever they happened to be (see p. 10). However, by the end of the 14th century the Court in all its aspects—administrative, judicial and parliamentary—had its headquarters at Westminster.

Although the Lords were from the first accommodated in the Palace, the Commons had no permanent meeting place of their own until the Chantries Act of 1547 abolished all private chapels. The most splendid of these, the Royal Chapel of St Stephen within the Palace of Westminster, had been founded by Edward I and finished by Edward III. As it was no longer used for worship it was handed over to the Commons, who had up to this time met in either the chapter house or refectory of Westminster Abbey. The Commons continued to assemble in St Stephen's until 1834, when the Palace was burned down. The fire destroyed almost the whole of the Palace of Westminster, except Westminster Hall, the crypt of St

Stephen's Chapel, the adjacent cloisters, and the Jewel Tower. The present Houses of Parliament were built over the next 30 years.

The Original Buildings

Westminster Hall is the second largest surviving medieval hall unsupported by pillars in Europe,[36] and is the oldest remaining part of the Palace. It is 73 m long, 21 m wide and 28 m high (240 ft × 68 ft × 92 ft) at its central apex. Its most outstanding feature is the hammer-beam roof, one of the finest pieces of wood-carving in Britain.

Westminster Hall was the great hall of the former royal Palace of Westminster and the site of a number of early parliaments, including the first true parliament, summoned by Simon de Montfort in 1265 (see p. 12). From the 12th to the 19th centuries the Hall was principally used as the regular meeting place for the Courts of Justice, and was the scene of many celebrated events in Britain's history. These include the state trial of Sir Thomas More in 1535, of Guy Fawkes and the other Gunpowder Plot conspirators in 1606, and of Charles I in 1649. It was also the scene of the depositions of Edward II (1327), Richard II (1399) and Henry VI (1461); and the proclamation of Oliver Cromwell as Lord Protector in 1653. The Hall was also used for great state ceremonies and coronation banquets from the reign of Stephen in the early 12th century to that of George IV in the early 19th. In more recent times it has been used for the lying-in-state of monarchs: Edward VII in 1910, George V in 1936, and George VI in 1952, and of statesmen: W.E. Gladstone in 1898 and Sir Winston Churchill in 1965.

[36]The largest is the Palazzo della Ragione (Il Salone) in Padua, Italy, which was built in 1219 and rebuilt in 1306.

The Hall is used today for major public ceremonial events, particularly when members of both Houses of Parliament need to be seated together. In 1977 it was the site of the presentation of the Loyal Addresses of Parliament to Queen Elizabeth II to mark her Silver Jubilee.

The Crypt. At ground level beneath St Stephen's Hall is another relic of the ancient Palace, the Chapel of St Mary Undercroft. Although the fire of 1834 destroyed the upper chapel of St Stephen's, the lower 'crypt' chapel escaped serious damage. It was built between 1292 and 1297, and from 1348 was served by a college of canons. After the dissolution of the college in 1547 the crypt was used for a variety of secular purposes, serving at different times as a stable, a coal cellar, and, for many years, as the Speaker's State Dining Rooms. In the mid 19th century it was restored, with elaborate gilding and painting, by Edward Barry (the son of Sir Charles Barry, the architect of the rebuilt Palace) to provide a chapel for the members of the two Houses.

The Cloisters to St Stephen's Chapel, to the east of Westminster Hall, were built in two storeys between 1526 and 1529. Both storeys, which are noted for their fan-vaulted ceilings, were restored on their original lines after the fire of 1834 and again after bomb damage in 1940. The storeys are connected by a wide stone staircase which provides the usual route to the Chamber for members of the House of Commons. Three sides of the lower storey are used as writing-rooms for members; the upper storey serves as a cloakroom.

The Jewel Tower, which stands opposite the Victoria Tower on the far side of Old Palace Yard, was built in 1365 to house the jewels and other personal treasures of the king. By 1621 it was used to store parliamentary records; it remained part of the Parliament Office until 1864, when the records were transferred to the Victoria

Tower. The Jewel Tower was restored in 1948–56 and since 1992 has housed an exhibition of the history of Parliament.

The Rebuilt Houses of Parliament

With the exception of the Commons Chamber, which was rebuilt after its destruction by air attack in 1941, the present Houses of Parliament are the work of the architect Sir Charles Barry (1795–1860) and his assistant Augustus Welby Pugin.

Barry's design, which incorporated Westminster Hall and the remains of St Stephen's Chapel, covers an area of over 3 hectares (8 acres) and cost some £2 million to build and furnish (about the same as the sum needed to rebuild the Commons Chamber alone between 1948 and 1951). It is a striking example of neo-Gothic architecture, designed to harmonise with the 13th-century Gothic style of Westminster Abbey across the road. The whole Palace is lavishly decorated both inside and out with the monogram VR (Victoria Regina, Latin for Queen Victoria, in whose reign the rebuilding was carried out), and with emblems of historic connections of the British royal family: the Tudor Rose, the pomegranate, the lily and the portcullis. The portcullis has become the emblem of the two Houses of Parliament. Much of the elaborate detail of the building, including the fittings and furniture, was the work of Pugin.

The approach to the Central Lobby of the Palace is through St Stephen's Hall (a passageway built on the site of the chapel and above the restored crypt) from St Stephen's Porch at the southern end of Westminster Hall.

The present St Stephen's Hall was built by Sir Charles Barry after the fire of 1834. It is on the site of the chapel, dating from

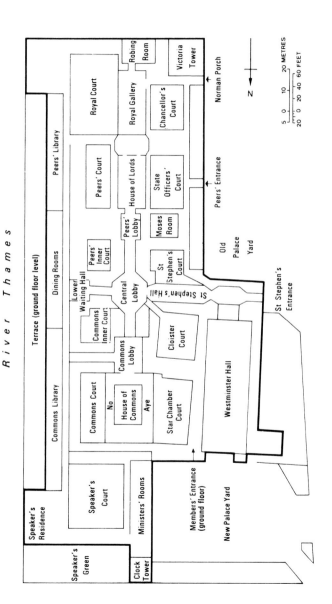

River Thames

Speaker's Residence

Speaker's Green

Clock Tower

Speaker's Court

Ministers' Rooms

Members' Entrance (ground floor)

New Palace Yard

Commons Library

Terrace (ground floor level)

Dining Rooms

Peers' Library

Commons Court

No

Aye

House of Commons

Star Chamber Court

Commons Inner Court

Lower Waiting Hall

Commons Lobby

Central Lobby

Cloister Court

Peers' Inner Court

St Stephen's Hall

St Stephen's Court

St Stephen's Entrance

Westminster Hall

Peers' Court

Peers' Lobby

House of Lords

Moses Room

State Officers' Court

Old Palace Yard

Peers' Entrance

Royal Court

Royal Gallery

Robing Room

Chancellor's Court

Victoria Tower

Norman Porch

N

5 0   10   20 METRES
20 0 20 40 60 FEET

1348, which for nearly 300 years served as the Chamber of the House of Commons. Marble statues of famous parliamentarians line the walls; these include Charles James Fox, William Pitt the Younger, and Sir Robert Walpole. There are wooden seats along each side of the hall for members of the public waiting to hear debates. Brass studs in the floor mark the position of the original Speaker's Chair and the Table of the House. The Central Lobby, a large octagonal hall, is the centrepiece of the building. Members of the public calling to see their MPs wait for them in this lobby.

From the Central Lobby, corridors lead northward to the House of Commons Lobby and Chamber and southward to the House of Lords. Beyond the House of Lords are the ceremonial rooms used at the State Opening of Parliament—the Queen's Robing Room and the Royal Gallery—reached by a separate entrance under the Victoria Tower. To the north of the House of Commons are the Speaker's and Serjeant-at-Arms' residences and various offices for ministers and officials. Beyond them is the Clock Tower housing Big Ben, the famous hour bell which came into operation in 1859 and weighs 13.7 tonnes (135 tons). The celebrated chime of the four quarter bells which precedes the striking of the hour is said to be based on a phrase from Handel's *Messiah*. A lantern shines in the top of the Clock Tower when either House is sitting at night and is extinguished when the Speaker leaves the Commons Chamber. When Parliament is sitting, the Union Flag flies from the top of the Victoria Tower from 10.00 until sunset, and when the Sovereign is present the flag is replaced by the Royal Standard (the Sovereign's personal flag). The Victoria Tower, one of the highest masonry towers in Europe and one of the three focal points of the roof of the Palace of Westminster, is now used to store some 3 million parliamentary records, nearly all of which may be consulted by the public in the House of Lords Record Office.

The 11 Palace courtyards lie to each side of the central buildings, separating them from the libraries, dining rooms and committee rooms on the east, facing the River Thames, and, on the west, from Westminster Hall and offices. The Speaker's residence is in the north-eastern corner of the Palace; New Palace Yard and the Members' Entrance lie to the north-west.

The existing buildings contain nearly 1,200 rooms, 100 staircases and over 3 km (2 miles) of passages. Additional accommodation for the use of the House of Commons has been built in Star Chamber Court to the west of the Commons Chamber, and for the House of Lords in a similar building in St Stephen's and State Officers' Courts. The Commons also uses other buildings in the area, including two seven-storey red-brick buildings on Victoria Embankment designed by the Victorian architect Norman Shaw, which were the former headquarters of the Metropolitan Police (known as New Scotland Yard). Construction work on additional parliamentary buildings to the north, across Bridge Street, started in 1987. Phase 1 of the scheme—the Parliament Street Building—was opened in 1991. It is the first purpose-built accommodation for the Commons since the inauguration of its new Chamber in 1950.

The public entrance to the Palace of Westminster is through St Stephen's Entrance in Old Palace Yard. The Royal Entrance is through the archway of the Victoria Tower, up the Royal Staircase. At the top is the Norman Porch which serves as an ante-room to the Robing Room; this opens onto the Royal Gallery, a processional room through which the Sovereign walks to the opening of Parliament. The Royal Gallery has been used for a number of parliamentary ceremonies and, in particular, for the reception of visiting statesmen and distinguished visitors. Among those who have addressed both Houses of Parliament here are Field Marshal Smuts in 1942; Prime Minister Kosygin of the Soviet Union in

1965; President Giscard d'Estaing of France in 1976; President Reagan in 1982; President Mitterand in 1984; the King of Spain and President von Weizsacker of the Federal Republic of Germany in 1986; and President Yeltsin in 1992.

The House of Lords

The Lords Chamber, the masterpiece of the rebuilt Palace, is more properly, if rarely, described as the Parliament Chamber, for it was primarily designed to provide accommodation for the Sovereign and both Houses when they met together for the State Opening. It was first occupied in 1847.

The Chamber is 24 m long, 14 m wide and 14 m high (80 ft x 45 ft x 45 ft). At its southern end is the Throne, from which the Queen reads her speech at the opening of Parliament; it is raised on steps which, when the House is sitting, are used as seats by Privy Counsellors and the eldest sons of peers as well as by members of the House of Lords.

In front of the Throne is the red cushion known as the Woolsack (see note, p. 29). Here the Lord Chancellor sits as Speaker of the House of Lords, and in front are two similar wool-sacks, used by judges at the opening of Parliament, and the Table of the House at which the Clerks sit. The Mace, a silver gilt orna-mental club of some 1.5m (5 ft) in length, symbolises the royal authority by which the House meets. It is laid on the Woolsack behind the Lord Chancellor whenever the House is sitting, except at the State Opening of Parliament when the Sovereign is present in person. The House of Lords has two maces, one dating from the time of Charles II and the other from the time of William III.

The Lords' benches, upholstered in red leather, are arranged on both sides of the House in five rows divided into three blocks;

The Chamber of the House of Lords

From an original drawing by Peter Heaton. Reproduced by kind permission of the House of Lords.

1 Throne	6 Clerks at the Table	11 Bar of the House
2 Woolsack	7 *Hansard* Reporters	12 Black Rod's Box
3 Judges' Woolsacks	8 Cross Benches	13 Press Gallery
4 Bishops' Benches	9 Government Benches	14 Strangers' Gallery
5 Table of the House	10 Opposition Benches	

the Government benches are on the right of the Throne, and the Opposition benches on the left. (Red, the traditional colour of royalty, has been the principal colour for upholstery in the Lords since at least the beginning of the 16th century.) The first two benches in the first block on the Government side are reserved for bishops. Facing the Woolsack below the Table are the cross-benches, used by members who do not belong to any political party. The lobbies in which the lords record their votes are on either side of the Chamber. There are also galleries on three sides of the House (see p. 53). The broadcasting authorities' commentary box is in the central part of the press gallery. Television cameras are positioned in opposite corners of the Chamber, and one in a side gallery.

The House of Commons

When the Commons Chamber was rebuilt after the Second World War, care was taken to preserve the essential features of Barry's building. However, the architect, Sir Giles Gilbert Scott, introduced many improvements; additional offices and better heating and ventilation were provided, and access to all parts of the House was improved. The new Chamber was completed in 1950; much of its furniture was given by countries of the Commonwealth. Barry's entrance to the Chamber, rescued from the rubble, was re-erected, still in its damaged state, and is known as the Churchill Arch.

The Chamber, like that of the House of Lords, is rectangular in shape, and its arrangements reflect the site of the Chapel in which it was originally housed. The Chamber is 21 m long, 14 m wide and 14 m high (68 ft × 45.5 ft × 46 ft). The Speaker's Chair stands on steps at the north end, and in front of it is the Table of the House at which the Clerk of the House and his assistants sit. At the head of the Table, whenever the House is sitting, rests the Mace of

The Chamber of the House of Commons

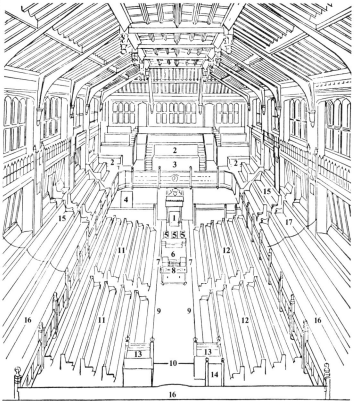

From a drawing by John Mansbridge. Reproduced by kind permission of the Rt Hon Mr Speaker, House of Commons.

1 Mr Speaker
2 Press Galleries
3 *Hansard* Reporters
4 Civil Servants advising Ministers
5 Clerks of the House
6 Table of the House

7 Dispatch Boxes
8 Mace
9 Lines
10 Bar of the House
11 Government Benches
12 Opposition Benches
13 Cross Benches

14 Serjeant at Arms
15 Members' Galleries
16 Visitors' Galleries
17 Gallery for Officers of the House

silver gilt, dating from the reign of Charles II. Like the one used in the Lords, it symbolises the royal authority by which the House meets.

The benches for members, upholstered in green leather, run the length of the Chamber on both sides, facing each other across a broad gangway known as the 'floor of the House'. (Green has been the principal colour for furnishing and fabric throughout the Commons since at least the mid 17th century.) The benches to the Speaker's right are used by the Government and its supporters; those to the Speaker's left are occupied by the Opposition and members of any other parties. The front bench on the Government side is known as the Treasury Bench.

There is no rostrum in the Chamber; except for ministers and spokesmen for the Opposition, who speak from the dispatch box placed on their side of the Table, MPs speak from wherever they have been sitting. On each side of the carpet running the length of the aisle is a red stripe, representing the point beyond which no member may step when addressing the House. The distance between the stripes is said to be that of two drawn swords. At the south end of the House is a formal barrier called the 'Bar'. It consists of two bronze rods which are normally kept retracted.

As in the old Chamber, seating accommodation for members in the new Chamber falls short of the total membership (651) of the House. The primary reason for this is to maintain the sense of intimacy traditional to the House of Commons. There are seats for 346 MPs on the benches and 91 in the centre side galleries.

The floor of the Chamber is overlooked by a series of galleries running round all four sides. The gallery above and behind the Speaker's Chair is known as the Press Gallery and is reserved for the official reporters who record for *Hansard*, and representatives of the British and foreign press, the BBC and ITN (Independent

Television News). Opposite the Speaker's Chair is the Strangers' Gallery, open to the general public and seating some 200 people, and there are also smaller galleries for officers, peers, guests and diplomats.

The broadcasting authorities' commentary box is on the floor of the House beneath the public gallery; eight remote-control cameras are mounted under the galleries.

The lobbies into which members pass to record their votes when a division is called are on the eastern and western sides of the Chamber. Members wishing to vote for a motion pass into the lobby on the right of the Speaker; those wishing to vote against it, into the lobby on his or her left.

Control of the Palace of Westminster

Control of the Palace of Westminster and its precincts was, for centuries exercised by the Lord Great Chamberlain; it passed to the two Houses of Parliament by agreement with the Crown in 1965.

The accommodation and services in that part of the Palace and precincts occupied by or on behalf of the House of Commons are controlled by the Speaker, advised by a select committee—the Select Committee on House of Commons (Services). In the House of Lords control is vested in the Lord Chancellor, who has handed over responsibility to a similar committee. Control of Westminster Hall and the Crypt Chapel is vested jointly in the Lord Great Chamberlain (representing the Queen), the Lord Chancellor and the Speaker of the House of Commons. The Lord Great Chamberlain retains his functions on royal occasions, and the Queen's Robing Room, with the staircase and ante-room adjoining, and the Royal Gallery remain under his control.

The Parliamentary Works Directorate (see p. 41) is responsible for the fabric of the Palace and for its upkeep.

Admission to the Houses of Parliament

When in session, the House of Commons sits from 14.30 on Mondays to Thursdays and 9.30 on Fridays. The House of Lords sits from 14.30 on Tuesdays, Wednesdays and most Mondays, from 15.00 on Thursdays and from 11.00 on Fridays at times of the year when business is heavy.

Visitors wishing to watch the proceedings from the Strangers' Gallery of either House should either obtain tickets well in advance (normally seven to eight weeks) from an MP or else join the appropriate queue outside St Stephen's Entrance. It is generally easiest to get in the House of Commons between 18.00 and 22.30 (or about 9.30 on Fridays). Overseas visitors may apply to their Embassy or High Commission for cards of introduction for admission during the afternoon; but such cards seldom ensure admission for Question Time.

Permits for guided parties to tour the Palace of Westminster and Westminster Hall can be obtained from Members of Parliament or Peers. Overseas visitors may approach the House of Commons Public Information Office (see p. 40).

The House of Lords Record Office is open for members of the public to consult the records of Parliament between 9.30 and 17.00 on weekdays and until 20.00 on Tuesdays when the House is sitting. Applications should, if possible, be made by letter or telephone (071 219 3074) at least 24 hours in advance.

Appendix 1
General Election 1992

The numbers of MPs elected in the general election of 9 April 1992 were as follows:

Conservative	336
Labour	271
Liberal Democrats	20
Plaid Cymru (Welsh Nationalist)	4
Scottish National	3
Ulster Unionist (Northern Ireland)	9
Democratic Unionist (Northern Ireland)	3
Social Democratic and Labour (Northern Ireland)	4
Ulster Popular Unionist (Northern Ireland)	1
Total	651

The total number of voters entitled to vote in the election was some 43.2 million, and 77.7 per cent of the electorate cast their votes—the highest turnout since February 1974. The percentages of votes cast for the main parties were:

Conservative	41.9
Labour	34.4
Liberal Democrats	17.8
Others	5.8

All 651 seats were contested and there were 2,949 candidates, compared with 2,327 in June 1987. The Conservative Party contested 645 seats, including all the 634 seats in England, Scotland and Wales and 11 seats in Northern Ireland. The Labour Party had 634 candidates, contesting all the seats in England, Scotland and Wales. The Liberal Democrats had 632 candidates, contesting all the seats in England, Scotland and Wales except two seats in England contested by Social Democrat candidates. The Scottish National Party contested all of the 72 seats in Scotland. Plaid Cymru contested all 38 seats in Wales; in three seats there were joint Plaid Cymru/Green Party candidates. The Green Party contested 253 seats and there was a large number of independent candidates or candidates belonging to other parties.

In Northern Ireland the Ulster Unionist Party contested 13 of the 17 seats, the Democratic Unionist Party 7, the Social Democratic and Labour Party 13, the Alliance Party 16 seats and Sinn Fein 14.

The distribution of votes among the main parties was:[37]

Conservative	14,093,007
Labour	11,560,094
Liberal Democrats	5,999,606
Scottish National	629,564
Plaid Cymru	156,796
Northern Ireland parties	785,093
Others	280,166
Total	33,504,326

[37]Figures supplied by the House of Commons Information Office.

The number of candidates who lost their deposits was 897, compared with 289 in June 1987. A full digest of voting at the 1992 general election (Factsheet No 61) is available from the House of Commons Public Information Office.

State of the Parties in the House of Commons in early March 1994

As a result of by-elections, the distribution of seats in the House of Commons in early March 1994 was: Conservative 330, Labour 266, Liberal Democrat 22, Plaid Cymru (Welsh Nationalist) 4, Scottish National Party 3, Ulster Unionist 9, Social Democratic and Labour 4, Democratic Unionist 3, Ulster Popular Unionist 1, Mr R Allason (from whom the Conservative whip has been temporarily withdrawn) 1, Vacant 4. Not included are the Speaker and her three deputies (the Chairman of Ways and Means and the first and second Deputy Chairman of Ways and Means), who do not vote except in their official capacity in the event of a tie.

An updated list showing current party strengths is published every week in the House of Commons *Weekly Information Bulletin*.

Appendix 2

By-elections and New MPs since the General Election of 1992

Constituency	Cause of by-election and size of former MP's majority	Date of by-election	New MP and size of majority
Newbury	death of Judith Chaplin (Con) 12,357	6.5.93	David Rendel (LD) 22,055
Christchurch	death of Robert Adley (Con) 23,015	29.7.93.	Diana Maddock (LD) 16,427
Rotherham	death of James Boyce (Lab) 17,561		
Barking	death of Jo Richardson (Lab) 6,268		
Eastleigh	death of Stephen Milligan (Con) 17,702		
Newham North East	death of Ron Leighton (Lab) 9,986		
Bradford South	death of Bob Cryer (Lab) 4,902		

Sources: House of Commons factsheet No 61: General Election Results, 9 April 1992
D.Butler and D. Kavanagh. The British General Election of 1992 (see Further Reading).

Appendix 3
Principal Officers and Officials

House of Lords

The Lord Chancellor
Chairman of Committees
Principal Deputy Chairman of Committees
Clerk of the Parliaments
Clerk Assistant and Clerk of Public Bills
Reading Clerk and Principal Finance Officer

Lord Chairman's Office
Counsel to the Chairman of Committees
Assistant Counsel

Public Bill Office
Chief Clerk
Senior Clerk

Judicial Office
Principal Clerk (Fourth Clerk at the Table)
Clerk
Judicial Taxing Clerk

Private Bill Office
Principal Clerk

Committee Office
Principal Clerk
Chief Clerk
Senior Clerks and Clerk
Second Counsel to the Chairman of Committees

Journal, Information and Printed Paper Offices
Clerk of the Journals
Printed Paper and Information Office Clerk

Record Office
Clerk of the Records
Deputy Clerk
Assistant Clerk

Official Report of Debates
(Hansard)
Editor
Deputy Editor
Assistant Editors

Establishment Office
Establishment Officer
Deputy Establishment Officer

Accountant's Office
Accountant
Assistant Accountant

The Library
Librarian
Deputy Librarian
Senior Library Clerk
Library Clerk

Black Rod's Department
Gentleman Usher of the Black Rod and Serjeant-at-Arms
Yeoman Usher of the Black Rod and Deputy Serjeant-at-Arms
Administration Officer
Staff Superintendent
Assistant Superintendent
Principal Doorkeeper
Second Principal Doorkeeper

Crown Office
Clerk of the Crown in Chancery
Deputy Clerk of the Crown

House of Commons

The Speaker
Chairman of Ways and Means
First Deputy Chairman of Ways and Means
Second Deputy Chairman of Ways and Means
Chairman's Panel
House of Commons Commission

Office of the Speaker
Speaker's Secretary
Trainbearer

Deputy Trainbearer
Speaker's Chaplain
Speaker's Counsel
Office of the Chairman of Ways and Means
Secretary to the Chairman of Ways and Means

Department of the Clerk of the House
Clerk of the House of Commons
Clerk Assistant
Clerk of Committees
Principal Clerks—
     Clerk of Public Bills
     Clerk of the Journal Office
     Clerk of the Table Office
     Clerk of Select Committees
     Clerk of Standing Committees
     Clerk of Domestic Committees
     Clerk of Financial Committees
     Clerk of Private Bills
     Clerk of the Overseas Office
Deputy Principal Clerks
Supervisor of Broadcasting
Senior Clerks
Clerks of Domestic Committees
Assistant Clerks
Editorial Supervisor of the Vote
Registrar of Members' Interests

Vote Office
     Deliverer of the Vote
     Deputy Deliverer of the Vote

Department of the Serjeant-at-Arms
Serjeant-at-Arms
Deputy Serjeant-at-Arms
Assistant Serjeant-at-Arms
Deputy Assistant Serjeants-at-Arms
Clerk in Charge
Admission Order Office
Principal Doorkeeper
Communications Manager
Parliamentary Works Directorate
Director/Deputy Director of Works

Department of the Library
Librarian
Deputy Librarian
Library and Research Services
Heads of Division
Heads of Section
Senior Library Clerks
Assistant Library Clerks

Finance and Administration Department
Director
Fees Office
Accountant
Deputy Accountant
Finance Office
Head of Office
Assistant Accountants

Establishments Office
Head of Office
Deputy Head of Office
Computer Office
Computer Officer
Network Planning Officer
Common Services Unit

Department of the Official Report
Editor
Deputy Editor
Principal Assistant Editors
Assistant Editors
Committee Sub-Editors
Reporters
IT Managers

Refreshment Department
Director of Catering Services
Operations Manager
Catering Accountant
Personnel Administrator
Catering Manager

Other Officers
Shorthand Writer to the House
Head of Security
Deputy Head of Security
Postmaster
Transport Manager
Director of the Parliamentary Office of Science and Technology

Appendix 4
International Parliamentary
Organisations

Two international parliamentary organisations, which bring together parliamentarians from all over the world and have branches in Britain, are described below.

Commonwealth Parliamentary Association

Founded in 1911 as the Empire Parliamentary Association, the Commonwealth Parliamentary Association (CPA), has evolved with the Commonwealth and now links together some 10,500 parliamentarians in 130 branches in legislatures in Commonwealth countries. Its main aim is to promote understanding and co-operation between Commonwealth parliamentarians and respect for parliamentary institutions. It pursues these objectives by organising annual Commonwealth and regional conferences, study groups, workshops, post-election seminars, and the exchange of parliamentary delegations. The Association is the only means of regular consultation between members of Commonwealth Parliaments. At its headquarters, in London, the CPA publishes a quarterly journal, *The Parliamentarian*, containing material on subjects of parliamentary and constitutional interest. Each issue also carries reports on important proceedings in many of the Parliaments of the Commonwealth. The Association also runs a parliamentary information and reference centre at 7, Millbank, London SW1.

Branches of the Association are formed by the legislatures of Commonwealth states, provinces and countries, and membership of a branch is open to all members of a legislature. In the United Kingdom branch full membership is open to current MPs and to members of the House of Lords. Former members may become associate members of the Association. The small secretariat of the United Kingdom branch is based in the Houses of Parliament and its Members' Room is in Westminster Hall.

Each year some 50 Commonwealth parliamentarians representing almost as many legislatures are invited to Westminster for a parliamentary seminar in March and a parliamentary visit in May. At the invitation of overseas branches the United Kingdom branch tries every year to send an equivalent number of its members on all-party parliamentary delegations to other Commonwealth countries.

Further information on the activities of the Association is available from:

The Secretary
United Kingdom Branch
Commonwealth Parliamentary Association
Westminster Hall
Houses of Parliament
London SW1A 0AA

(Telephone: 071-219 5373)

Inter-Parliamentary Union

Founded in 1889 on the initiative of a British MP and a French Deputy, the Inter-Parliamentary Union (IPU) was originally seen as a means of achieving international arbitration. It has since developed into the only worldwide organisation of parliamentarians. With a current membership of 129 parliaments, the Union seeks to resolve disputes by peaceful means and to promote the ideals of democratic government. IPU representatives reflect the broadest range of political and ideological differences. They meet at half-yearly conferences and at other special meetings when parliamentarians can debate issues of international concern.

The Union's international secretariat is based in Geneva. It implements decisions taken at Conference, assists national groups in their activities, and issues the *Inter-Parliamentary Bulletin* four times a year.

Under the supervision of an all-party executive committee, elected annually, the British group of the Union comprises over 500 MPs and 300 members of the House of Lords, with the Lord Chancellor and the Speaker of the House of Commons as Honorary Presidents and the Prime Minister as President. As well as ensuring appropriate representation at the annual conferences, the British group organises visits by foreign parliamentary delegations to Britain and visits by British parliamentary delegations to foreign Parliaments, and promotes bilateral contact through some 50 affiliated parliamentary groups.

Further information on the British group of the Union is available from

The General Secretary, British Group
Inter-Parliamentary Union
Houses of Parliament
London SW1 0AA   (Telephone: 071-219 3011)

Appendix 5
The Council and the Cabinet

From the 13th to the 17th century the monarch in England turned principally to his or her council, which developed from the Curia Regis, for advice on administration and for the implementation of policies. Certain royal officials were almost always members of the council. They included the Justiciar (the leading official for two centuries after the Norman Conquest), the Chancellor (who emerged as the leading royal officer at the end of the 13th century), the Treasurer and the Secretary (later Secretary of State). The council in 1526 (by then known as the 'Privy Council') included, for instance, the Chancellor, the Treasurer, the Secretary, the Lord Privy Seal, the Earl Marshal, the Lord Chamberlain, and certain officers of the King's household, together with other dignitaries, lay and ecclesiastical. Government policies and legislation were laid before Parliament by those Privy Counsellors who were members of Parliament. Until the 16th century the Privy Council usually had 12 to 20 members; it later increased considerably in size.

By the seventeenth century the Privy Council had become a large and unwieldy body, some of whose members held sinecures or posts carrying little or no administrative responsibility. As a result a committee system was developed. Committees of the Privy Council had existed for various purposes from the 16th century, and some of these evolved departments of State. From 1660 the appointment of committees responsible for both special and regular business was a recognised procedure. Almost inevitably one of the committees came to be recognised as the most influential, although this might vary from time to time, according to the relative importance of internal or external affairs. The increased size of the council after 1660 had another result: the King began to seek advice from individuals and smaller groups within the Privy Council rather than consulting the entire council or its committees. The smaller inner group to whom he gave his special confidence was variously known as the 'Junto' (a term first used during the reign of Charles I), the 'Cabal' (after the initial letters of the inner group of 1671—Clifford, Arlington, Buckingham, Ashley and Lauderdale), the 'Cabinet Council' or the 'Cabinet' (the cabinet being the private room or closet of the King's palace in which the group met).

After the Revolution of 1688 the Privy Council continued to decline in influence. By the time of the accession of the first Hanoverian monarch, George I, in 1714, it was generally recognised that the Privy Council—now the Privy Council of Great Britain—had been superseded as the effective governing body by the Cabinet of men holding high office in State, Church, or royal household. The formal link with the council was (and still is) that all members of the Cabinet were members also of the Privy Council. The meetings of the Privy Council lost their importance as the Cabinet became the recognised centre of affairs. Instead sessions of the council (except for the summoning of the full council upon occasions such as the accession of a new monarch) were confined to recording business needing formal certification.

The 'Inner' Cabinet

As with the Privy Council, so with the Cabinet: a distinction developed between the whole body (which included such dignitaries as the Archbishop of Canterbury and the Master of the Horse) and the 'inner' or 'efficient' Cabinet containing ministers who enjoyed the particular confidence of the King and who were able to secure a majority in Parliament for his policies. An inner Cabinet was clearly in operation when Sir Robert Walpole was chief minister (1721–42) but it was not until after 1783 (when William Pitt the Younger became leading minister) that the composition of the Cabinet came to be confined to the ministerial heads of the principal departments of State and the holders of traditional offices (for instance, Lord President of the Council, Lord Privy Seal), who were, in effect, ministers without portfolio. The principle that a member of an outgoing Cabinet had no right to sit in the next Cabinet was not established until 1801. A few years after the accession to the throne of George I in 1714 the monarch ceased to attend the meetings of the inner Cabinet, but he continued to preside over, the rare meetings of the full Cabinet, which discussed matters such as the contents of the King's speech opening a session of Parliament.

The Prime Minister

The leading position in the Cabinet came to be associated with the Treasury, and the name 'Prime Minister' was first applied to those who held office as Lord Treasurer or—after the Lord Treasurership had been placed in commission in 1714—First Lord (Commissioner) of the Treasury. The Treasury had, as it still has, a predominant role in government because of its control of the public purse. At that time the Treasury was also responsible for dispensing royal patronage which, before the formation of modern political parties, was the main element in maintaining a government majority in Parliament.

The reigns of the first two Hanoverian monarchs (who were also Electors of Hanover) saw the development of an administrative authority separate from the King—in the chief 'Prime' minister. George I (1714–27) and George II (1727–60) still held ultimate executive power even if they did not exercise it directly: their agreement was essential for the formation of a ministry and its continuance in office. Although Sir Robert Walpole is often referred to as 'the first Prime Minister', he did not enjoy a position independent of royal favour. Instead, what collective responsibility his ministry possessed was due to the strength of Walpole's personality; when he fell from power his ministerial colleagues did not resign with him. George III (1760–1820) himself exercised direct political control in the first part of his reign. But with the progress of reforms which limited the possibilities of rewarding supporters in Parliament with royal patronage, the long ministry of Pitt the Younger (1783–1801 and 1804–06), and the King's attacks of mental illness, George III played a diminishing role as his reign proceeded. Sir Robert Peel, Prime Minister from 1841 to 1846, was probably the first minister to occupy a position closely resembling that of a modern Prime Minister. By this time the Reform Act 1832 had started the process which eventually led to universal adult suffrage, and, by implication, to direct popular control over the House of Commons. Since the late 19th century the Prime Minister has normally been the leader of the party with a majority in the Commons. The monarch's role in government is largely limited to acting on the advice of ministers who are responsible to the electorate, through the House of Commons, for their policies.

Further Reading

The British General Election of 1992.
Butler, David and Kavanagh, David   Macmillan   1992

The Commons under Scrutiny.   Routledge   1988
Ryde, M. and Richards, P.G. (editors)

The House of Lords. Shell, Donald   Philip Allen   1988

Consititutional and Administration Law.
Smith, S. A. De, Street, H. and Brazier, R.
Sixth revised edition.   Penguin   1990

The House of Lords. Shell, Donald   Philip Allen   1988

*The Houses of Parliament: A Guide to
the Palace of Westminster.*
Fell, Sir Bryan and Mackenzie, K. R.
Fifteenth edition, revised by
D. L. Natzler   HMSO   1994

How Parliament Works. Silk, Paul (with
Walters, Rhodri)   Longman   1989

*Member of Parliament: The Job of
a Backbencher.*   Macmillan   1990

*Parliamentary Practice (A Treatise on the Law,
Privileges, Proceedings and Usage of Parliament)*
Erskine May, Sir Thomas. Twenty-first edition,
edited by Clifford J. Boulton.   Butterworth   1989

The New Select Committees.   Oxford University Press   1989

Electoral Statistics Annual   HMSO

Whitehall and Westminster: Government

Informs Parliament: the Changing Scene.   Longman   1985
Workings of Westminster.
Englefield, Dermot   Dartmouth   1991

Ombudsman: Jurisdiction, Powers and
Practice.
Clothier, C. M.   Manchester Statistical Society   1981
Parliamentary Companion. Annual
     Dod's Parliamentary Companion Ltd.

Parliament: Functions, Practice and
Procedure. Griffith, J. A. G.
and Ryle, Michael.   Sweet & Maxwell   1991

Parliamentary Companion. Vacher's
Four issues annually. A. S. Kerswill

Parliament and Congress.
Bradshaw, Kenneth and Pring, D.   Quartet   1982

Parliament Today. Adonis, Andrew
     Manchester University Press   1990

Representation of the People? Parliamentarians
and Constituents in Modern Democracies.   Gower   1985

The Times Guide to the House
of Commons, April 1992. Wood, Alan and Wood, Roger (ed)
     Times Books   1992

Aspects of Britain series

British System of Government   HMSO   1993

The Monarchy   HMSO   1991

Organisation of Political Parties   HMSO   1994

Parliamentary Elections	HMSO	1991
The Civil Service	HMSO	1994
History and Functions of Government Departments	HMSO	1993
Britain's Legal Systems	HMSO	1993
Pressure Groups	HMSO	1994

Factsheets on various aspects of the House of Commons and its work, including lists of MPs and ministers, are available free from the House of Commons Public Information Office.

Factsheets on various aspects of the House of Lords and its work are available free from the House of Lords Journal & Information Office.

Annual Reports

The House of Commons Commission. Annual Report.	HMSO
Parliamentary Commissioner for Administration. Annual Report.	HMSO
Standing Orders of the House of Commons 1989–90 (Public Business).	HMSO
Standing Orders of the House of Lords (Public Business).	HMSO 1989

Index

Printed in the UK for HMSO.
Dd.0297872, 5/94, C30, 566734, 5673.

TITLES IN THE ASPECTS OF BRITAIN SERIES

The Monarchy

Parliament

Parliamentary Elections

Organisation of Political Parties

Ethnic Minorities

Women in Britain

Britain and the Commonwealth

Human Rights

Honours and Titles

Criminal Justice

Britain and Hong Kong

Energy and Natural Resources

Religion

Northern Ireland

The British System of Government

Planning

Education

Britain and Africa

Agriculture, Fisheries and Forestry

Sport and Leisure

Employment

Britain in the European Community

Conservation

Transport and Communications

Britain's Legal Systems

The Aerospace Industry

Britain and the Gulf Crisis

Overseas Relations and Defence

Social Welfare

Wales

Scotland

Housing

The Arts

Immigration and Nationality

Pollution Control

Britain and the Falkland Islands

Britain and the Arab-Israeli Conflict

Broadcasting

History and Functions of Government Departments

Telecommunications

Britain, NATO and European Security

FORTHCOMING TITLES

European Union · Britain's Overseas Trade · Pressure Groups